INTRODUCING ERIK ERIKSON

An Invitation to his Thinking

Francis L. Gross, Jr.

UNIVERSITY
PRESS OF
AMERICA

LANHAM • NEW YORK • LONDON

Copyright © 1987 by

University Press of America,® Inc.

4720 Boston Way
Lanham, MD 20706

3 Henrietta Street
London WC2E 8LU England

Printed in the United States of America

British Cataloging in Publication Information Available

Library of Congress Cataloging in Publication Data

Gross, Francis L.
  Introducing Erik Erikson.

  "List of books and films": p.
  "Books and articles by Erik Erikson": p.
  Includes bibliographies and index.
  1. Developmental psychology.   2. Self.
3. Erikson, Erik H. (Erik Homburger), 1902-
I. Title.
BF713.5.G76   1987   150'.195'0924   86-29025
ISBN 0-8191-5788-0 (alk. paper)
ISBN 0-8191-5789-9 (pbk. : alk. paper)

To Toni, my wife,
To Joseph and Matthew, my sons,
Who have taught me even more
about human development
than Erik Erikson

ACKNOWLEDGEMENTS

Grateful acknowledgement is made to W. W. Norton and Company, Inc., New York, for permission to quote from Erik H. Erikson, <u>Young Man Luther</u> (1958), <u>Identity: Youth and Crisis</u> (1959), <u>Childhood and Society</u> (1963, 2nd edition), <u>Dimensions of a New Identity</u> (1974), <u>Toys and Reasons</u> (1976), <u>Insight and Responsibility</u> (1964).

CONTENTS

FOREWORD

This is a book that is meant to inspire, to incite, or even to drag its reader to read and think about the work of Erik H. Erikson. It consists of ten excursions into Erikson's writing. It may be read by itself. It may be read better if the reader concomitantly reads the suggested readings in Childhood and Society that are indicated at the end of each chapter. Since Childhood and Society is Erikson's book, it will give the reader of this book a chance to decide whether or not this work of mine is helpful in understanding what Erikson has to say himself.

A reader working more in depth would do well to delve into Erikson's other books: I have indicated which parts of his other books are especially apropos for each chapter of this book. Each chapter's suggested readings contains as well a series of apt novels, plays, poems, and films, plus a very slim set of recommended technical readings by authors other than Erikson.

If this book is used as a text for class, I strongly recommend at least one novel, play, film or set of poems for each chapter, along with the suggested readings in Childhood and Society. A psychological system without a story, after all, is like eggs without salt, or worse, salt, without eggs. The literary suggestions should salt the eggs. Conversely, I cannot resist noting that some of these suggested adventures in literature would surely "egg" the reader on to a deeper understanding of Erik Erikson's thought.

This writer himself has been encouraged and helped (I hesitate to continue the egg metaphor further) by many people. I am reminded, writing in their debt, now that most of the writing is finished, how much I owe them. In no particular order then, my thanks to Ann Trompeter and Cynthia Rugenstein who proofed and typed. To Stephanie Groshko Grathwol, who put an unruly manuscript in order on a very magical word processor. To the undergraduate students in my class who studied and criticised an early version of this manuscript as a part of their course requirement in GSSC 121, Dimensions of Human Behavior, at Western Michigan University. To Professor Nita Hardie who taught that course with me. All together, I think of

them as "All the king's horses and all the king's men
and women" who kept this particular Humpty Dumpty from
taking a great fall while he frequently teetered on his
perch composing this book.

FRANCIS L. GROSS, JR.

Western Michigan University
Kalamazoo, Michigan
September, 1984

PART ONE

INTRODUCTION

CHAPTER I

THE GROUNDPLAN OF PSYCHOSOCIAL DEVELOPMENT

A. Reasons for Writing this Book

This is a book about Erik H. Erikson. It is meant to be, as you might have gathered from the title, an introduction to Erikson's writing. It is my hope, as the author of this book, that it will lead the reader to Erikson's own work. I have written this book because I would have liked to have had a plain-spoken, no nonsense, book-length introduction to Erikson's work when I first read Childhood and Society fifteen years ago.

In the years since then, I have seen many a student lose her way reading Erikson. Reading Erikson is like walking in a dense and beautiful forest with a thousand paths leading through it. The very richness of the forest can be confusing. There is so much there. The books themselves have not been published in a neat and logical progression. They are records of their author's own developing interests. They are written for the general public, it is true, but Erikson has never watered down or simplified his writing on that account. Thank God! They are written with a kind of magnificent obscurity. The reader sometimes feels that he is coming in at the middle of a book, when in fact, he is at the opening page. Indeed, some things are assumed...but what are they? Erikson possesses, furthermore, a dazzling vocabulary. He is at home in literature of several languages-- Danish, German, and English, not to mention Latin and Greek. He is conversant with an amazing variety of academic fields. He is conversant with embryology, anthropology, sociology, theology and philosophy, besides his chosen field. All these fields are a part of his palette, if one thinks of his books as paintings. His work needs to be read and reread; his books need to be outlined and meditated on. They have a lasting quality. The problem is getting started. There is that haunting feeling that you really never know enough to start.

The density, the complexity, the refusal of the author to simplify, and I must admit, that other quality which I have inadequately described as "magnificent obscurity"--all these have contributed to my own brash assumption that I can write a book about

Erikson's thinking that is, in some sense, clearer than his own expression of what he thinks. I mean to write this book <u>plainly</u>. If I succeed, it will be because I have been plain. Let us begin.

B. E. H. E.: Man and Psychoanalyst

Who is Erik Erikson? What sort of man is he? Erik Erikson is a healer. His primary concern is with a person's soul. That rules out the kind of concern your family doctor has for health, which we will assume, is primarily a concern for your bodily health. Erikson's concern for your soul is different as well from the kind of concern your local priest, minister or rabbi might have. They are likely to be concerned with your relationship with God. The Greek word for soul is "psyche;" it is with the health of your psyche that Erikson concerns himself. Some people would call him a psychologist, but it would be more proper to call him a psychoanalyst. This is the term that Sigmund Freud used for the practitioners of his own original kind of healing.

As a young man in his late twenties, Erik Erikson was hired to teach the children of the people studying psychoanalysis in Vienna under Freud himself. Erikson had never been to college; he was an artist, who proved to have an exceptional knack of dealing with children. This gift of his was noticed by Anna Freud, Freud's daughter and colleague. She asked the young teacher if he were interested in becoming trained there under her her guidance, as a psychonalyst. And so it came to happen, almost casually, that this young man, over a period of six years, became a psychoanalyst. He never lost his interest in children; he never went to college in later years; and he never put aside a fundamental cast of mind that is artistic. If you would understand his work, you must remember these last three things.

During the time when Erik, whose name at that time was Erik Homburger, was teaching the children of the married people studying psychoanalysis in Vienna, he met a young woman of Canadian-American descent, Joan Serson; they fell in love, married in Vienna, and had two sons there, Kai and Jon. In all, Erik Homburger spent six years in Vienna. At the end of this time, he and his family moved from Vienna, after a short stay in Denmark, to Boston, Massachusetts. The year was nineteen thirty-three, Adolph Hitler had risen to power in Germany and was menacing Austria; it

4

was well known that Hitler had little use for Jews; and less use for the new form of psychology known as psychoanalysis. Young Herr Erik had just graduated from the Vienna Psychoanalytic Society. He, like the founder of psychoanalysis, was a Jew. It was time to go.

There were contacts in Boston that seemed promising for his career; his wife's homeland beckoned. By Christmas of nineteen thirty-three Boston had the Erikson family ensconced in the New England winter; America had its first child psychoanalyst; Erik was a distinguished immigrant.

This is not a biography, but it is meant to be an introduction to the work of Erik Erikson. He himself would be the first to say that a full understanding of a person's thought, or even an introduction to it, needs be accompanied by something of the person's life story.

C. Freudian Theory

Back to the theory. We have established Erik Erikson as a follower of Sigmund Freud's new theory and practice of psychoanalysis. It is not surprising that this school of thinking, this way of healing a person's troubled psyche, grew and changed as the followers of Freud grew to maturity themselves. Freud's great basic insights remained with them, but there was plenty of work to do in the infant science.

1. The Unconscious

It was Freud who in our time opened the minds of men and women to a vast area of a person's mind that lies hidden to consciousness. He envisioned the human spirit much as one might imagine an iceberg, only a small part of which is visible to the human eye. Much of human activity, Freud felt, was governed by motives of which an individual was unaware. Under the thin skin of the conscious mind was a seething caldron of desires and thoughts frequently at odds with one another, rooted in the experience of early childhood in the family, and often the cause of emotional upset later. Freud's shaft of light into this dark underpart of the human mind came about through the analysis of dreams, the use of hypnosis, and the listening carefully to the talk of his patients as they, without any attempt at planning, spoke of

5

themselves in a random, but revelatory manner known as free association. A person's recovery from conflicting emotional pulls was brought about primarily by that person's coming to an understanding or insight of her own previously unconscious motives. What then was Freud's chief means of healing? Neither drugs nor medicines, not surgery, nor any of the other commonly used means of the medicine of his day. When a patient <u>understood</u> what was beneath the surface of her suffering, therein lay the cure.

The roots, as Freud saw it, of distress in a person's spirit, lay in childhood and relations with mother and father during infancy and childhood. Freud became infamous in his day, shocking to his medical colleagues and to the Victorian world at large, with his insistence that in large part these early conflicts were sexual in nature. Small boys were seen by Freud as actively sexual and involved sexually with their own mothers. The process of coming to terms with the fact that they would never replace their own fathers as primary lovers of their mothers was seen by Freud as a matter of great importance in freeing children in later life to be able to form unions with women other than their own mothers in sex and marriage. By the same token, small girls desired their fathers and had to learn to accept the powerful rival for father's affections, their own mothers. Young women had to satisfactorily accept defeat in their first love affair and to identify with their former rivals if they, too, were to be able to have healthy heterosexual relationships on reaching maturity. The fact that these infantile experiences were part of the unconscious of the average adult, coupled with the prudery of the Vienna society of Freud's day, made his statements about infantile sexuality's relationship with adult turmoil all the more sensational.

2. Psychosexual Stages

If Sigmund Freud revealed humankind's unconscious mind to a world which thought then that conscious motivation and conscious thought were all that there was to a person's spirit, psyche or soul, this was only the beginning.

Freud saw the life of a newborn child as developing not just in the unfolding by stages of the psyche in conjunction with the body. A newborn infant's center of attention, both sexual and

6

otherwise, was his mouth. The sucking of the nursing infant was the world's center for him or her. At the end of its second year the child's focus of attention changed from mouth to anus; a child held on to her feces or expelled them in either rage or joy as the mother attempted to train her to be regular in her habits. The young three or four year old was seen by Freud to be centered around the phallus or vaginal opening as he or she was openly "on the make" for mother or father. Later came a period of sexual latency encompassing the remaining years of childhood to the time of puberty. At this time, with the coming of adulthood, came the last of the psychosexual stages, called genital, in which once more one's sexual drive became activated as the basis of a mature sexuality. So, not only do we have an unconscious mind, but we have a regularly developing, changing, shifting pattern of growth.

3. The Id

Freud's focus on the unconscious concerned sexuality and the family. He regarded each person as a battleground of opposing forces. A person lacking the enlightening experience of psychoanalysis was seen by Freud as unaware of most of this struggle. What were these forces? Consider all the powerful and primitive drives existing in each of us...the drive to be angry and fight, the drive to become sexually aroused and to have sex, the drive to become fearful and run away, each in all the thousands of ways they can be nuanced and expressed. Freud summed up these drives in a single word which English translators of his work call the "id".

4. The Superego

Then consider all the prohibitions, all the "no-nos" one must learn and internalize from infancy through childhood. And we underline here the word "internalize". For although attitudes of the propriety of civilized life are often learned consciously, they do become "part of us" so that we are no longer aware of their governing power. Babies learn sensual restraint, or the lack of it, while nursing; they later learn to control their bowels and urethra with greater or lesser rigidity; and still later they learn who is and who is not fair game sexually. Most of these attitudes are internalized and just disappear from our awareness. Lumping together the restrictive attitudes

7

one has, treating them as a whole, gives birth to the Freudian word "superego".

5. The Ego

How was a person to deal with these two opposing parts of herself? Was there no restraining influence? Yes, says Freud, a person does learn to keep some sort of personal order within. One has a sort of power of referee, a power to moderate, even to synthesize the dictates of one's primitive desires as they war with the "civilized" or restraining forces within. When the starving man part of me looks at a sirloin steak, it wants to pounce on the steak; it urges me to snatch it right off the serving dish with my hands and stuff the whole thing in my mouth; another part of me urges moderation, taking just a small part, waiting my turn, using the knife and fork, chewing with my mouth shut, sitting in a chair like a lady or gentleman. How can I survive in polite society and at the same time preserve any zest in the joys of eating steak? There is a part of me whose function it is to somehow weave the opposing forces together into a single, harmonious pattern. Be it noted, that Freud himself had a rather pessimistic view of the power of this refereeing part of a person. By and large he felt that civilization's growth in a person was to the detriment of those lusty drives. Or, the lustier and healthier those drives, the less civilized the person. The poor old referee or synthesizer was generally not effective in giving to each of the other parts of the self a sort of artful unity.

The sketch given above is felt necessary in an introductory work such as this, because it seems to this author that the reader should be reminded that even an introductory knowledge of a post-Freudian demands some knowledge on the part of the reader, of the Freud from whom the post-Freudians come. This writer is willing to remind his readers of this, but he is unwilling to do more than glance in Freud's direction, because of the strictures of a short introduction.

D. Erikson's Contribution

What are the uncharted areas of psychoanalysis which Erik Erikson has found himself drawn to expand into?

1. Societal and Historical Factors

Erikson has wryly noted that he, following the
lead of Anna Freud herself, feels that "the ego has
quite a bit more on its hands than the id." And what
does that mean? It points to the limitations of a
psychoanalysis that contents itself with influences in
a man or woman's life limited to father, mother and
siblings. The title of Erikson's first book is
Childhood and SOCIETY.* The definition given to
Erikson's stages in human growth is psychosocial, in
distinction to Freud's psychosexual stages. Erikson's
early work among the Sioux and Yurok Indians showed his
concern for a wider dimension than the family in early
childhood influences. He became acutely conscious of
children as growing up in a particular society which
itself dictated norms, however unconsciously, to its
parents as regards early childhood training. Sioux
children from infancy were prepared to be a warrior
people, accustomed to privation and pain and condi-
tioned to sharing their goods with one another as their
migrant form of life demanded. Yurok babies were
trained from infancy to be retentive rather than
sharing, to be savers rather than warriors, keepers
rather than sharers.

Erikson observed that Sioux babies in the nineteen
forties were being cared for by their mothers with
little if any change from the days in which the Sioux
followed the great herds of buffalo. During this same
period, government agents were trying to get these
people to settle in one spot, to become ranchers and
farmers. Erikson's study of contemporary Sioux customs
of baby care is a study in irony. It shows clearly how
futile the effort of well-meaning white reformers were
for the Sioux. It underlines as well how deeply
imprinted a human life becomes in babyhood and early
childhood. The social worker didn't get to the Sioux
until, male and female, their basic bent in life was
already set.

The Yurok, on the other hand, did quite well in
adapting to a society that wanted them to save money
and compete for this world's goods. It has been no
great leap for a basically retentive people to switch
from catching and storing salmon to catching and
storing dollars. In both cases, the role of tribal
society is a powerful one in family life. If Erik

(*Emphasis mine.)

9

Erikson began to insist on seeing the development of the person as _social_, he at the same time insisted that every society exists in a historical moment. If the basic Freudian insight that a man or woman's personal history, specifically childhood, has great bearing on what kind of an adult that person might turn out to be, then reasoned Erikson, the societal history of an individual's tribe or nation will have great impact as well. If my people have historically been buffalo hunters or Puritans or slaves or revolutionaries, that history is going to be reflected in me, whether I recognize it or not.

2. Freud and Erikson: Writers

It is at this point that I would remind the reader of another point in common between Sigmund Freud and Erik Erikson. Both are healers as we have noted, with a peculiar method of healing...that of insight. There are, in the history of any people, many gifted, insightful, and generous men and women who concern themselves with the healing of wounds of body or spirit. The vast majority of these people content themselves with the skillful practice of their art or science. Only a few put in writing what they have learned. Freud was one of these, a writer as well as a psychoanalyst, and so is Erik Erikson. It is doubtful whether either of them would be as vital as each is in the world of psychology today had they not given us detailed accounts of what they have seen as well as a theoretical framework enabling them to put order into their discoveries and hand them on to others.

3. Adult Stages

And so we can see in writing the psychosexual stages of human development as Freud saw them. We can see as well, in the writings of Erikson, the historical and societal dimensions added to the stages of Freud. Furthermore, Freud seems to have left human development complete with the arrival of adult sexuality following adolescence. The forty years or so of adult life that one can expect in today's world were left uncharted. Erikson not only complicated the Freudian scheme of development, he extended it to cover the entire span of an individual's life, which he calls "the life cycle." He is the forerunner of contemporary developmental psychologists who deal in detail with human development of a person in her thirties and forties, her fifties, and sixties, and even the developments that occur in the approach of death.

4. A New Ego

He is one of a number of thinkers in psychoanalysis, headed by Freud's daughter Anna, who was
Erikson's own analyst, one I say, who has put more and
more stress on the importance of the ego. If Freud's
idea of ego was that of a rather feckless rider on a
runaway horse, Erikson and other "ego psychologists"
not only see the ego as having societal and historical
issues to deal with, along with and in company with
family issues, he also sees the ego as a potentially
active synthesizing power in a person. The ego part of
an individual is the part that makes an identity out of
all the identifications a person has experienced. It
is the power to make something of one's self. The
ingredients of childhood, history and society are given
to a person; each person has an individualized set of
potentials unlike any other person. Out of these
ingredients a person must make some kind of blend,
skillfully or badly. There is a power of choice here,
much of it unconscious. It must be seen, however, that
as Erikson sees it, the choice is always limited, and
continuous throughout life. In a certain sense,
everyone is a "self-made person." In another sense
nobody is. This is because what I become will always
be an expression of my family, my people, my childhood,
my past life, and the history of my people. It will
always be affected by the times in which I actually
live and the places in which I live those times.
Lastly, if Erikson and Freud are correct, I will always
be an expression of the body in which I live.

5. The Body

If I am human, I will always be some-body, and
not just any-body either. Throughout the centuries of
Western thought, religious and philosophical thinkers
have warred among themselves over the importance of
the body in the human person. Some see a human being
as a spirit imprisoned within a body, weighed down, as
it were by an inferior partner, the real world being
the world of the spirit rather than the material or
bodily world. The body then is despised and looked
down upon; it is not a thing of beauty or dignity; it
is a lower principle and its drives for pleasure are
"lower" and interfere with the "higher" life of the
spirit. We cannot restrict such an attitude to such
ancients as Plato, the Gnostics and the Christian

Manichees. Certainly, in American history, the Puritans were affected by such a spirit as were a large part of the Irish immigrants who came after them. For both, bodily pleasure and beauty, especially sexual desire, were considered evil. Coming closer to our own time, the so-called Playboy philosophy of sex is a subtle form of Puritanism, for it glorifies sex as nothing more than play, robbing sexual love of its profundity, its beauty and its power to form a lasting union between woman and man.

Erik Erikson is no Puritan. His insistence on the unity of soul and body puts him in the camp of the writers of the Jewish scriptures as well as Christianity's gospels and the letters of St. Paul. Soul and body are one in the Hebrew Torah as well as the Christian Scriptures.

It is only with the advent of Greek thought to the Hebrew and Christian world that we get the fatal division of humankind into body and soul, with the body frequently getting short shrift in dignity and beauty. Christianity's roots are in Hebrew thinking; the coming of God's son as a human being is a profound compliment to the bodily side of humanity. If Freud has been accused of sexism in our day, it is not because he took bodies too seriously; it is very likely because he did not take the bodies of women seriously enough in the rich differences that separate them from their brother, man. So would Erikson argue in the years after Freud's work was complete. This book will treat Erikson's attitude toward male and female in a later chapter.

E. Further Aspects

1. Artist and Observer

If an introduction to Eriksonian theory seems to become more and more theoretical, let me remind the reader and myself that Erik Erikson is an observer and an artist more than he is a logician with a nice neat way of looking at human beings. He has no unified and encompassing theory. He has rather a keen set of observations and a series of sketches of human behavior, all of which are intended to be of use in the healing of the human spirit. It is important to remember that he is always the artist; it is equally important to remember that he is equally intent on healing the divided heart of man and woman. His chief

12

means, as we have said before, is understanding insight.

2. Insight, Transference, and Cure

A word further on psychoanalytic insight. We left the patient on the couch free-associating ideas and feelings in the presence of the unseen analyst. The analyst listens, and watches the client, looking for indications of hidden conflicts, anchored in the client's past. Part of the psychoanalytic theory of healing is that the client or patient talks about the person or persons in the past who slowly come to light as the source of later emotional turmoil. In the process of this talking, the person under treatment unknowingly treats the analyst the same way as the person in the past. Suppose for example, my father had beaten me frequently when I was a small boy and that in later years I found myself cringing and paralyzed by the presence of my boss at work; my discussion of my distress at work in analysis would lead slowly back to my father. In the ideal order I would unknowingly then treat the analyst like my father. I could "work through" my childhood fears by in a sense having a second chance to encounter my long-deceased father in the person of the analyst. This process can lead to an understanding of the irrational fears I have of my boss and a consequent change of attitude on my part. The endowing of the analyst with another person is called "transference." Transference is not limited to analysts, of course.

Erikson himself describes how Martin Luther, who had had an abusive father, evened the ancient score with his Dad, when in later years, he thumbed his nose as a reformer to the Pope of Rome. (The word Pope means "father"; the Italian word is "papa".) He got away with it too, beginning as he did so, the great groundswell movement in Christian history known as the Reformation.

Put another way, Martin Luther needed to come to terms with a father who had abused him as a child. At this moment in history Martin's church was corrupt and in need of reform. The Pope, then as now, was a father figure for the Church. If Martin managed to settle an old score with his father by taking on the great "Papa" of his church, we can see both transference and genius in Luther's action. Having an old score to settle added depth and vigor to the dirty job Luther

as a church reformer. It is the task of the
/st to take on the healing burden of
:e of patients who are unable to make these
:es on their own. Luther managed <u>his</u> father
in the pope more than three hundred years
before Sigmund Freud was born.

3. History and Biography

This introduction has made passing reference to
Erik Erikson's concern that the dimension of history
is an important one in understanding any person or
group of persons. What I have not mentioned is the
fact that Erikson has undertaken two major biographies.
One of these, which I have made use of above, is a
biography of the Father of Reformation Christianity,
Martin Luther. The other concerns itself with Mohandas
Gandhi and his use of militant nonviolence. The por-
trait of Luther concerns itself with Luther's struggle
for his own Identity as a young man, illustrating at
one and the same time Erikson's Identity theory, which
we will treat in a later chapter, and also how Luther
himself can be understood both through hints given in
his own writings and from the record of the biographies
of others, much in the same way a psychoanalyst
understands a patient. Mind you, the psychohistorian
is not afforded the luxury of having his subject "on
the couch", nor is a life study necessarily a study of
what went wrong with a person, as a case study is. A
life history, as Erikson sees it, is a study of larger
dimensions; it is more concerned with how a person
managed to put his life together rather than focusing
on breakdown and upset, i.e., how a person managed to
fall apart.

If Erikson's study of Luther can be read with
profit by anyone concerned with Youth, his study of
Gandhi centers on Gandhi's middle years and how he
became father and mother to the modern State of India.
This book is a study of how a middle-aged man managed
to care for his country as a mother or father cares
for a child, carrying this concern not alone to his
own Indian people, but to the British occupying forces
and other enemies of the common Indian as well. His
gentleness and respect for life as used in politics is
traced to his childhood and youth, so that the reader
can see with the eye of both historian and psychoanalyst the origins of militant nonviolence as they
existed in one man, in a particular time of history and
in a peculiar set of personal circumstances. Erikson

has brought his clinician's eye to bear on other important figures of history and fiction, ranging from Hamlet to Hitler, treating the old man in Ingmar Bergman's classic film, <u>Wild Strawberries</u>, the playwright George Bernard Shaw, Thomas Jefferson, William James and others.... always with an eye to a wider understanding on the part of persons who have lived after the subject of the biography. We will see more of Gandhi and Jefferson in later chapters.

F. Psychosocial Stages

And so, the Eriksonian concern with history... history in its broad sense, encompassing peoples and civilization and times and places, always with the intent of understanding the individual person as she or he stands on this or that soil during this or that age of the world. If history is at the heart of Erik Erikson's work, the history of the individual is at the heart of this heart. Erikson's psychosocial stages, encompassing the history of a given individual, stand as one of his greatest contributions to his field and have been a help for understanding the self by both professionals and ordinary people who simply want to understand themselves better.

What better witness of this latter have we than the ten years Erikson himself taught a General Education course for undergraduates at Harvard College entitled, The Life Cycle. His students were not required to be on their way to degrees in the social sciences. They were in search, many of them, of a Bachelor of Arts degree. The course they took was part of the Liberal Arts or General Education requirement. It was a popular course, because it spoke to the search of self understanding that is part of the search of youth in any time or place.

In the five chapters that follow this one, I shall attempt to explain the famous eight stages of Erikson's Life Cycle.

1. Embryological Roots; Epigenesis

As we move, then, toward the paradigm for a single person's history, let us see how Erikson's model came to be. He tells us that he borrowed his model of development from the science of embryology, the study of the development of the fetus. The word embryologists use for fetal development is "epigenesis". Its adjectival form is "epigenetic". Erikson borrowed this term in his description of human development after birth.

The embryologists Erikson studied found the animal fetus to develop in a certain regular order which could not be reversed or changed without doing damage to the fetus itself. Each organ of the fetus has a time of ascendancy, a time when it would take form. If, say, the heart of the embryo normally developed and took form before the liver and after the brain, then if its development took place in a different order or in a slower sequence or time, or, for that matter, a faster rate, then not only is the heart likely to be malformed, but the organs following it in sequence also stand a chance of malformation; for their time of ascendancy will have been changed. Put another way, each stage in the development of the embryo affects each other stage in the timing and sequence of development. An interruption or aberration at the beginning will not only affect the life of the organ in the process of growing and taking form, it will affect the regular growth and formation of all the other organs of the embryo. One could picture a jigsaw puzzle that not only had interlocking pieces, as all jigsaw puzzles do, but added to this a requirement that the puzzle's parts must be put together in a certain sequence and with a certain speed in order for the parts to fit together properly to produce a whole picture.

Erikson borrowed a model of development from studying the embryo, but he used that model with modifications to show how human beings develop after they have been born. Such a borrowing is not the scientific use of embryology but a very ingenious application of the principles of embryology in another sphere. This is an artistic use of a model, useful not because the growth of human beings after birth follows exactly the growth of the embryo, but because using these principles happens to shed light on a very complicated growth and development process. Artists have always borrowed what they needed from other disciplines in order to give life to their pictures and sculptures. And so, we remember Erikson the artist.

Erikson has observed a certain special time, a certain crucial time, for the development of certain human qualities. His first stage in psychosocial

16

development is a time in which the newborn baby has as a primary concern a struggle within itself between trust and mistrust. The normal outcome of this struggle between two opposing qualities in the newborn will be an attitude of hope. This time, the first year of life, is the optimum time for this basic strength of hope to be established. Following the analogy of the epigenetic growth of organs in the embryo, Erikson notes that this basic strength can continue to develop throughout the life of the person. Put another way, the struggle between basic trust and mistrust will, in later stages of life, continue in a more mature way, but its special time, necessary for all future normal development, is at the beginning, the first year of a baby's life.

2. Crisis

A word about the way in which each stage is named. Erikson sees each stage of life as a time of creative tension between two opposing forces within a person. For him, all of life consists of a struggle, or, as he puts it, each stage of human life is marked by a crisis. The term "crisis" is used not primarily to denote impending disaster, but rather in a positive sense, a necessary turning point, a crucial moment...

When development must move one way or another, marshalling resources of growth, recovery, and further differentiation.

The first crisis in human living, then, is a crisis of trust. It is important to see that Erikson sees this time, not as one marked by basic trust on the part of "good" infants or by mistrust on the part of less fortunate babies. It is precisely the experience of both that marks this time. It is Erikson's hope that trust will predominate in the struggle. Still, there can be no trusting without the experience of its counterpart. And the counterpart has a positive role to play. This is like saying that you can never be a brave woman or man until you have experienced cowardice. Until you have run away in the face of danger, played the coward, you will never really know what bravery is, nor will you ever be truly brave. So, in Erik Erikson's descriptions of different stages of life, every one of them is marked by a struggle of one kind or another. His is not a view of human living, in which a person ever "has it made" or has found her "niche." Niches are reserved for statues, not living persons. Being alive at all means being involved in a struggle to grow, a struggle that does not end until life itself is over. Key to his kind of thinking is noting that all life may be a struggle, all right, but as one grows older, the struggle has different forms, different foci, different concerns.

Also key to this way of looking at life is the realization that each stage is built on the ones which have preceded it. If the second stage in an infant's life is marked by a struggle between autonomy and shame or doubt, the outcome of that struggle depends a great deal upon the establishment of an attitude of trust or hoping. The battles of the past thus remain the supports or the weaknesses of the battles of today. It is as if we carried each stage with us as we go along in life, for good or for ill.

3. Continuity

Hence Erikson's insistence upon what he calls "continuity" in a person's life. Continuity is a difficult notion to get hold of, but it has to do with being in touch with where one has been before. Tragedy is seen in a person who has not only lived through childhood, but who in adult years retains nothing of that initial hope, playfulness and other qualities that were once hers. It is the task of the ego to blend previous identifications into the self in an artful and creative manner. The ego is the blender of past and present. If one's past is buried, it is difficult to get on with the blending.

If this is true for a person's personal history, so is it also true for a person's awareness of the history of her people, her nation, her race. The past of my people is also my past. The most powerful reason for being in touch with my history is that a part of me is there, a part that would remain inactive and unused, and above all, not understood in myself, were I not aware of it. Being in touch with one's history, whether personal or in a wider sense, makes continuity possible in myself as an interesting, productive and moral human being.

From this point then, in this chapter, which is an introduction to a book that is an introduction, we look forward to a more detailed presentation of the eight stages of human life that are the receptacle of each person's history and which provide a sort of map through the times of life by which one may learn a sense of continuity in that life.

As we are poised at the point of beginning a detailed presentation of the stages of the Life Cycle, it would be well to remind the reader that it is always assumed in Eriksonian psychology that life is a balancing act. A person's faculty for achieving a working balance of body and spirit at a point in one's history which is both personal and societal -- this faculty is called the Ego. Any discussion of stages in human life involves balancing and synthesizing. There is always a tension, always a struggle. It is the ego's task to blend a personal unity of all these forces. The ego is at the heart of all Erikson's stages. The ego is in the middle of the counterplayers of each stage. Failure to achieve a working balance is ego failure.

The presence of the ego is so pervasive in an Eriksonian view of life that it becomes taken for granted, and as a consequence, both reader and writer can overlook its centrality. Erikson's own descriptions of life stages use the word "ego" sparingly, as do the descriptions in this book. Such is its pervasive quality. These words are to remind the reader that without a person's capacity to blend and balance the forces in and around her, this psychology of balance and growth would make no sense at all.

RECOMMENDED READINGS FOR CHAPTER ONE

Should the reader find herself in the situation of knowing that, despite good intentions and high motives, she will likely only read one of Erik Erikson's books, I recommend the first one, Childhood and Society.

It is a great classic in its field; Erikson himself has never surpassed it as an expression of the general outline of his work. The second edition is revised and normally would be the one to get. The first two chapters of this book could be read with profit at this point in one's reading of Introducing Erik Erikson.

Childhood and Society contains an excellent report on Erikson's work among the Sioux and Yurok Indians. The reference is, Part Two: "Childhood in Two American Indian Tribes." He has an entire book on Martin Luther's youth, entitled Young Man Luther. The material on Luther in this chapter is taken from that book. Lastly, Erikson has done a biography of Mohandas Gandhi, with emphasis on Gandhi's mature years. It is entitled Gandhi's Truth. References to Gandhi in this chapter are taken from that biography.

All of Erikson's books give the reader a general grounding in his system of thinking. His most recent book, The Life Cycle Completed (A Review), gives a careful placement of its author within the world of psychonalysis. There are many psychoanalysts, beginning with Freud. Where Erikson finds his own contribution and what is special about his work is described in the first chapter. The fourth chapter elaborates his understanding of ego, society, and history. A thorough treatment of the key notion of "epigenesis" is found in the second chapter.

Of Erikson himself there is no full-scale biography. Robert Coles' very readable book, Erik H. Erikson, The Growth of His Work, is the story of how Erikson's work grew. Since the man cannot be separated from his work's development, there are inevitably details of Erikson's life. Coles is a reliable observer. Neither Erikson's work nor his life were completed when Coles wrote this book. Erik Erikson is alive and productive at this writing. His age: eighty-two.

Later chapters of this book will recommend readings in literature--plays, poetry, novels. This first chapter, however, is so broadly theoretical as to make "illustrations" from literature cumbersome and artificial.

PART TWO

THE LIFE CYCLE

CHAPTER II

CHILDHOOD (STAGES ONE THROUGH FOUR)

A. Stage One: Trust vs. Mistrust

1. Mother and Child

We begin at the beginning, the first year of a
child's life, characterized, as we have seen by a
struggle between basic trust and mistrust. Think of a
baby, unable at first, even to roll from back to
stomach, helpless. Think of this infant looking
upward into the eyes of the mother or mothering figure,
bent over the child, holding it, changing it, rocking
it, and nursing it. Recall the rich sounds a baby
makes while nursing, the deep satisfaction as it
noisily takes its milk. All is well with the world
while it nurses, is rocked, is crooned and sung over.
There is a heavy sense of bodies in this bond between
mother and child, the mother enfolding the baby,
surrounding it, making up for the lost womb in which
the infant was before birth, establishing a firm basis
for trust.

Erikson has himself noted that the paintings and
sculptures of Madonna and Child covering the entire
span of the Christian era celebrate this bond between
mother and infant, as a sort of cornerstone or fundament of life. Contemporary researchers have shown the
disastrous results for infants who have not been held
or rocked by mother or mothering figure. Hospitals
working with premature babies in incubators have discovered that food and warmth are not enough to sustain
the life of a newborn child. Being held and rocked are
just as important.

Think of the rage, as only babies can rage, when
this numinous figure takes time out for the rest of her
life, the screams of outrage at being wet, hungry, or
just without mother. What mother or father has not
learned that there comes a time when the harried grown
folks realize that you can't rock the baby all night
every night. Sometimes you have to let them yell.
Parents must live too! Somehow enough trust must be
established between the two so that the baby can wait
for her coming, supine and helpless, trusting that she
will indeed return. This is the fundament of babyhood, the establishment of a basic strength called
hope, through the interplay of presence and absence,

of a deep satisfaction centered around the infant's mouth, suckling, gurgling, or wailing the loss of nipple and milk--out of this mixture of anger and satisfaction we hope for the foundational virtue of hope, for the rest of human life.

There is a schematic view of the eight stages at the end of this book in Appendix C. This is a slightly modified version of a presentation done by Erikson himself in <u>Youth: Identity and Crisis</u>. The eight stages are represented in a diagonal line from the bottom left hand corner running to the top right hand corner of the diagram.

2. Later Forms

If the first year of life is the time of ascendancy and special concern for trust and mistrust, we must remember , that this most fundamental tension will remain, hopefully marked by a predominance of hope, in different forms at each of the later stages of human life. It is not just established forever, like a cornerstone in a building. No, it is alive right through life, and developing.

I have seen a small boy left to his own resources for a moment, disappear into an open doorway to visit people he had never seen before, so convinced he was that the whole world was his friend. His mother, who had provided him with that great sense of trust, has grown gray hairs ever since, knowing as she does, that not all strangers are trustworthy.

What high school teacher has not been aghast at the trust placed in her or him by an adolescent she has known only for a few months. Suddenly, there are the confidences of youth in her lap, a strange assurance that she will be able to explain it all or heal the wound.

The great lovers of humankind, the Gandhis and Mother Teresas, are the grown children of mothers who taught them to trust at infancy. A parent who stubbornly refuses to give up hope for his children. An old woman who can look death in the eye and still hope for something more. The trust of these people has its origins in infancy.

3. Societal Aspects

Should the reader think, from this short description, that there is a sort of blueprint for the first year of life, a sort of rigid pattern or behavior for mothers, to be adhered to come hell or high water, it is then time to remind the reader of the dimension of society in this stage. Different mothers or maternal persons, in different times and societies, follow different patterns in the first year. Erikson has noted the lavish attention given by Sioux Indian mothers to babies as preparation for the generosity needed among a wandering people, each of whom is so dependent on the other for the goods of hunting, the spoils of battle, the sharing of fortune and misfortune. How different the other tribal group studied by Erikson, a people who were more sedentary than the Sioux, more acquisitive, more "capitalistic"--the salmon fishers of the West Coast, the Yurok. These people weaned their babies after six months. No more breast-feeding after that, a rather dramatic demonstration that you'd better not trust your neighbor too much. After all, it's a competitive world. Not surprising that the Yurok have adapted to the world of business better than the Sioux. As for contemporary mainstream American habits for infants, the reader can draw her own conclusions as to whether we prepare our life for a competitive society, a capitalistic world, or not.

B. Stage Two: Autonomy vs. Shame and Doubt

1. Terrible Twos

With the beginnings of a child's second year, we have a gradual shift in concern. In terms of the language of the body, a child is often standing up now--and standing up to the big people, father and mother. The beginnings of a sense of being someone separate, unique. Families who have never heard of Erik Erikson have learned by observation to call this time in a child's life the "terrible twos." Why so terrible? The word Erikson uses is "autonomy." A good synonym for autonomy is independence. The word "willful" applies here. Among other things, the word "willful" connotes being obstinate and headstrong, having a mind of one's own.

I have a vivid memory of a two year old boy down the block from my home, standing on the porch and

27

pounding his chest with his fists while shouting to all the world, "Mine-a, Mine-a, Mine-a, Mine!" The world was his, and anyone who wanted any part of that world that he wanted had better look out! We are not just speaking of freedom here, but a beautiful (and sometimes terrifying) conviction of omnipotence. "The world is my onion and I deserve it!"

Someone once asked me what word my children used most often at this stage. That was easy to answer. The word was, "No."...not "Mamma" or "Dadda", but "NO!" I still have a vivid recollection of my two year old son smearing his own feces on the wall adjacent to his crib at nap time...not just once, but two days in a row! This a traditional toilet training time in some cultures...and that brings up shaming.

Although the word "shame" is used commonly in English, Erikson uses it so precisely, that it would be well to dwell on it here. Shaming has to do with the exposure of a deed or a part of one's self...a part you want to keep covered, or a deed you'd just as soon nobody knew about, like wetting your pants.

I might add that shaming is not restricted to parents. I remember well the ridicule heaped on a very small boy by other neighborhood children when they discovered him incautiously relieving himself in his own backyard. That was his last outdoor pee for a long time. Every culture uses shaming to some extent to keep its "deviates" in line; our own uses it to train children to "hold it" while not on the toilet and to "let go" only on what is aptly called, in the United States, "the throne." Many a battle has been fought with a willful two year old and his parents over just when and where to let go...and so, to socialize them, to "civilize" them, we shame them.

When you get caught with your hand in the cookie jar, you are being shamed. Spanking is a form of shaming. So is being sent from the table in front of everyone. Small children try to "cover up" when caught, let's say trying to sneak an extra piece of cake in the kitchen. Sometimes they literally cover their faces with their hands, thinking you won't be able to see them.

I saw a two year old hurl himself on the floor after knocking a pitcher of water off the kitchen table in his house. He was trying to cover up his act by hoping to disappear through the floor!

The sister of shame is doubt. As Erikson uses the term, it concerns the part of myself that I cannot see, which produces a product on command and in a certain place. How can I be so praised for "doing my job" on the toilet and yet so shamed for using my product for finger painting. I have a dark and sinister side, out of sight.

Doubt is concerned with what I cannot see. I cannot see my own face, except in the mirror. Is it pleasing? I can't smell my own breath or see my rear end. If I learn to be afraid of what I cannot see in myself, that is doubt. If I learn a sort of assurance that the things about me which are invisible or unknown to me are bound to be good and worth-while, beautiful or strong, <u>that</u> is autonomy; that is pride.

2. Later Forms

If I become fixed upon such self-doubt about this hidden dimension, in later years I shall be doubtful and suspicious of every dark corner, every insufficiently known newcomer, every new movement...indeed anything, anyone, any place that is not well-known to me. Or, I can become tragically self-conscious, ashamed of myself, my figure, my face, my feet, my color, my sex. Indeed, a culture may teach me, at this early age, to "hold on"...in order that I may later be able to save money or guard my property, or at least to "keep my shit together." Picture a teenaged girl whose breasts are too big, she thinks...or too small, or too distressingly normal. Or a boy of seventeen who won't go swimming, because he is six feet tall and weighs only a hundred and thirty pounds. Or a woman of thirty who <u>has</u> to be told she is beautiful every hour. Or a teacher who is terrified of student questions.

Perhaps you have noticed areas in your own life where you really are "at home" and at ease. You remember a summer when you never worried about what your body looked like in a swimming suit. Or a course in high school where you could answer <u>any</u> question without fear. Or a friend you are at ease with.

Autonomy and pride, shame and doubt, begin early all right. But the tussle between them lasts your whole life; what you hope for is a line of development in which you have more autonomous and prideful times than shameful and doubting ones.

3. Societal Aspects

Societies which, like the Sioux, place no great value on where and when one goes to the pot, find their adults less retentive in their attitude towards possessions. The old migratory Sioux form of life demanded a kind of sharing, a kind of socialism among its people...and they began preparing for this form of generosity early.

Different societies put a premium on different kinds of letting go and holding on in their babies. But some form of positive willfulness, some form of determination to be independent, my own person, standing on my own feet, is the hoped for strength to emerge from the battle between autonomy and shame or doubt. The self-sufficient and generous Sioux warrior, the householder in suburbia with the neat-as-a-pin house and manicured lawn...both are products of a stage in life modified carefully, if usually unknowingly, to fit a given society. Adults in any society reflect, one way or another, the pride or shame they learned as toddlers.

C. Stage Three: Initiative vs. Guilt

1. Big Wheels

And where do they go from the terrible twos? In the threes and fours, the years remaining before formal schooling begins; in our society, there is usually a remarkable maturing of motor control, a sort of all-round blossoming characterized by the ability to run or to master tricycle or big-wheel, together with the ability to mimic adult behavior in games and play. This is an age of "get up and go." Erikson uses the word "initiative."

How well I remember a four year old boy who jumped aboard his big wheel tricycle one summer morning and went careening down the sidewalk from our house on the corner. He tore all the way down to the next corner, made a sharp left turn with the zest of a racing driver, and darted down the sidewalk to the next corner. Only then did he look back--and there was no familiar house on the corner to reassure him. His newfound speed had run him clear out of his own world. I found him in the dirt under a bush, sobbing and woebegone. "You lost me!" he said.

Another four year old adventurer disappeared out
of the back door of his house that same summer,
leaving no trace for his soon frantic family.
Relatives and neighbors were called, and finally the
police, who scoured the neighborhood. At five P.M. he
suddenly appeared at that same door, as if by magic,
greeting his tearful mother with bravado. "I went to
see grandma," he said, "but the son of a bitch wasn't
in!"

This is the age of play and drama. It is an age
when the seeds of infant trust, sown at the very
beginning of life, take the form of play. In play,
children's make-believe games can come out the way the
kids wish every battle would come out, with them on
top. There is endless rehearsing for future roles, and
endless changing of the ends of lost battles. Erikson
says that play performs the task in children that
dreams and daydreams do for adults. They provide hope,
a field for practice, and a way to adjust to painful
situations that cannot be avoided.

A younger brother came proudly home from
kindergarten with a beautiful finger painting of a
monster of terrible proportions, a sword-like object
sticking in the monster's ample belly. "Who's the
monster," I asked. Without batting an eye he gave his
elder brother's name. In finger painting the often
vanquished become victors--even over elder brothers!

In the sexual arena, this is the age when active
boys are "on the make" for their own mothers, while at
the same time aware of the long shadow cast by Dad on
their most fervent efforts. This is likewise the age
when girls realize that they have overwhelming rivals
in their mothers for the affection they feel for their
Dads. Children of this age are frequently sexually
active in lots of ways. Such a shock it is to parents
to find little Billy with Pam from the house down the
street giggling in the bathroom without a stitch of
clothes between them!

Three year old Georgie reached up from his place
on his mother's lap, lustily grasping one of his
mother's breasts. "No, George," she yelped, "That
hurts!" A moment's thought on George's part led to a
modest proposal. "Can I just pet it?" he asked.

31

The counterplayer of initiative is guilt. If shame comes from being caught, guilt differs from it in that one can feel guilty <u>without</u> being caught. Guilt arises from the <u>fear</u> of being caught. It is the voice of conscience, the voice, as it were, of the unseen God. The imagination of the child can invent terrifying monsters; the dream of being a lover to one's opposite sex parent can bring with it the fear of being caught by the powerful rival, the other parent. There are all sorts of dreams in which a child can be terrified for having gone too far. The monsters and goblins of Maurice Sendak's books for children, which are so frequently thought of by adults as totally foreign to the world of children, are quite familiar to kids of this age; most of them recognize these monsters, tamed by being on the pages of paper, and hence safe, fascinating, and of course, familiar. The guilt of this period is the beginning of conscience, of responsibility, to become a crippling monster if the parent, the model for this conscience, fails to live up to it himself in the eyes of the child. Hypocrisy in important adults is devastating to a child, confusing, crippling, and paralyzing.

2. Play: Key to Survival

Ordinarily, these youthful moralists survive their moralism and in later life become ethical rather than woodenly moral. The key to survival at this stage is play, just as in later life a sense of playfulness is the key to a genuine ethical sense, one that is neither wooden, rigid, or punitive. Playfulness allows a sense of purpose to survive, the ability to act, to set about getting something done.

3. Societal Aspects and Later Forms

As for societal differences in a sense of initiative or purposefulness, one can contrast the chief figures in Erikson's two major biographies. Mohandas Gandhi's powerful leadership in India in the first half of this century was characterized by his own sense of right and wrong, his reverence for human life, his respect for the British Occupational Forces, all this embodied in a childlike playfulness that teased the British Lion unmercifully. Gandhi's militant non-violence had its roots both in Indian culture as well as English law...an amalgam of various societal values. He had a very Indian sense of purpose.

32

We have seen how Martin Luther, the great religious reformer of European Christianity in the sixteenth century, had a conscience formed in part by a brutal patriarch, his father. This father's physical abuse of his son in the setting of the Saxon family of the day, a father-dominated family, set the scene for a reformer who wanted very much to settle a score with Dad as well as one who settled the hash of a corrupt papacy. Martin Luther's conscience drove him to do the dirty work of reform with a zest, a vigor and a vengefulness that would have been unlikely, had it not been for the ill treatment he received as a child from a "papa" who did not live up to the strict morality he enforced on his family. And so we have at one and the same time examples of consciences formed by society as well as family, and a picture of how these two great moralists were both affected in later years by the consciences of their childhoods. Gandhi, of course, was a tease as a child, a family favorite, spoiled, and allowed considerable freedom in his favored position as the youngest of a large family. He was a playful experimenter all his life; the reverence of his mother for his own small world as well as the worlds of the large group of related children all living under one roof in that extended family was not lost on Gandhi then or later, when he put the inviolacy of human life to work in the political arena. The child was father of the man of great purpose. The child is parent of all persons of purpose as well as those whose later years are without it.

D. Stage Four: Industry vs. Inferiority

1. Workers

And so, the advent of school, so formal a preparation for later life in our society, but present, however informally, in the years before puberty the world over. Learning the skills of adulthood, the three Rs. Children at this stage, called the latency stage by Freud, put aside their fantasies of sexual prowess and many other prowesses. They put aside a life dominated by play and go to work. Those who work successfully do not lose a sense of playful initiative, a playful purposefulness. Their sense of autonomy and pride is not only a residue from earlier years; it is alive and with a new nuance. An attitude of hope has new scope, the hope for success in studies. A new and larger world, then, the world of school and identification with school's tasks. Schoolchildren who can

33

read, do their arithmetic, and write are generally happy children. Those who cannot, feel inadequate and inferior to the others. Of course, as in all of Erikson's stages, reader and non-reader exist in the same child, young mathematicians and those who despair of ever being able to add a sum correctly coexist in the same child. Ink-smeared and hopelessly crossed out papers, in contrast with flowing penmanship and clear sentence forms, come from one and the same child. We do not have, for the most part, a world of "either or" but a struggle between two. Still, it is no surprise that truants and delinquents in our society are likely to be the ones who can't read, write or add. The resultant strength? One might guess it; it is competence.

I worked as an assistant for a number of years at Boys Industrial School in Topeka, Kansas. The school was a state-run correctional institution for boys of grade and high school age who had repeatedly run afoul of the law. The psychologists on the staff freely admitted that one of the most effective people they had in the entire institution was a woman who taught remedial reading to the boys. Many and many a kid learned to read in that school under her motherly eye. A very healthy percentage of her students never again had serious trouble with the law again. Illiteracy, the source of their terrible anger and frustration, was gone. Competency in reading keeps a lot of kids out of jail.

2. Societal Aspects

The societal aspect of this stage is nowhere clearer in the writings of Erik Erikson than in his description of the failure to draw real involvement from the children of the Sioux Nation in the white man's school system. The stoic apathy in most students in the face of years of schooling underlines that the three Rs, so basic to success in White America, are not the skills that the Sioux people felt they needed to succeed in their dream of returning to the old nomadic life, hunting the buffalo on the great Midwestern Prairie. The same programs that challenged white American kids to work or feel inferior had little effect one way or the other on the children of the Sioux of the nineteen forties. Although not successful for the most part, they did not show the symptoms other American children would show as the accompaniment of failure in class. Sioux society just did not recognize

34

the worth of the schools of another society, a society which they refused to adopt as their own.

3. Later Forms

As for later manifestations of this stage, one can point in the cases of both Gandhi and Luther, to a moderately successful primary school life, setting the stage for the period of youth that was to follow, for more sophisticated skills, so that, later still, each of these giants of their own times would take the skills of work learned in childhood and adolescence and put them to uses never dreamed of by their teachers. Luther, as a thoroughly trained priest and monk, would take on the church hierarchy of his day, using his store of knowledge to fight for the freedom of the individual conscience, as no outsider could have. His very training was a powerful weapon in his preaching and writing against the church that trained him.

Gandhi's early schooling, which did not foreshadow his greatness, laid the foundation for his going to England to study law as a young man. It was out of a law practice in South Africa that the young Gandhi made his peculiar political tool for the liberation of India. The young Gandhi emerged as a Hindu who saw the Hindu reverence for life with the eyes of a lawyer trained in British Law. He brought nonviolence from the private sphere into the public arena of politics and made it a powerful weapon for India's struggle for independence from Great Britain.

Gandhi used his basic skills in a way that no school teacher or law professor ever dreamed of. Like Luther, he took the skills at hand and used them to defeat the very system at whose hands he had been a student. Gandhi the Schoolboy was a real parent to Gandhi the Law Student, who in turn gave birth to Gandhi, the Father and Liberator of India.

The young Luther, studying his Latin in school, gave rise to the precocious but sorrowful young monk, who in turn developed into the angry reformer who tossed Rome and things Roman out of the churches of Germany, returning them to the German language and to the individual consciences of the German people. Without basic skills, there would have been no Mahatma Gandhi nor would there have been the Luther who provided the spark for the Reformation.

35

Here ends our treatment of the first four of Erikson's stages, the stages of childhood. We will move, in the chapter following this one, to the often tumultuous years of the time between childhood and adulthood, the time of youth. This is the time of the formation of each person's individual Identity, a time in life described by Erik Erikson with a skill and sensitivity surpassed by no social scientist of this era.

RECOMMENDED READINGS FOR CHAPTER TWO

I would refer the reader of this chapter to Erikson's first book, Childhood and Society. Chapters Three and Four concern the Sioux and Yurok people. Chapters Five and Six are concerned primarily with children. Chapter Seven contains a description of the stages of childhood.

A more venturesome reader might foray into Young Man Luther. Besides showing how Luther the Reformer emerged from the babyhood and childhood of Little Martin, we have what I consider Erikson's most brilliant description of Youth, the stage described in the next chapter of this book.

Gandhi's Truth provides an excellent picture of how Gandhi the Man emerged from the playful child and earnest youth who preceded Gandhi's adulthood. This book provides the fullest treatment Erikson gives of mature adulthood, his seventh stage.

For an overall view of the eight stages of the life cycle, I would recommend the really remarkable feature-length film, Everybody Rides the Carrousel, by John and Faith Hubley. This is an animated film, very dense in its content, worthy of a number of viewings. The visual scenes of people at each stage remind this reviewer that Erikson himself began as an artist rather than a purveyor of words. These are brilliant sketches of each stage.

I would further recommend that the reader make excursions into the world of literature for an understanding of Erikson's stages. I do not here intend a complete list, but a sampling. Maurice Sendak's Where the Wild Things Are is a marvellous story of the vaulting imagination of a small boy. Mordecai Richler's Jacob Two Two Meets the Hooded Fang is a beautiful humorous tale of a boy at the beginning of stage four. Jennifer, Hecate, MacBeth, William McKinley, and Me Elizabeth by E. L. Konigsberg is a good stage four story as well. You will have your own favorites from your own reading. At the back of this book is a complete list of all the books and films mentioned in this book, with publishing dates and authors, should you wish to find one or another of these books.

CHAPTER III

YOUTH (STAGE FIVE): IDENTITY VS. IDENTITY CONFUSION

A. The Crisis of Identity

1. A Definition?

It would be sensible to begin a chapter on youth and Identity with a nice, neat definition of what is meant by the term. We begin by waffling. Youth is the time in life that begins with the advent of puberty and ends when adulthood begins. The problem, of course, is "When does adulthood begin?" We could get into further hot water by saying that adulthood begins when Identity is established. Identity, as Erikson himself will tell you, is an important concept, but, for Erikson at least, it allows no pat definition. Erikson, it is important to know, was the theorist who first gave the term Identity meaning in the social sciences. He is the coiner of the term "Identity Crisis." If he is chary of being too neat in defining these terms, we must respect that. We can do no better at this point than to quote him on Identity Crisis, where he is most succinct:

> I have called the major crisis of adolescence the Identity Crisis; it occurs in that period of the life cycle when each youth must forge for himself some central perspective and direction, some working unity, out of the effective remnants of his childhood and the hopes of his anticipated adulthood; he must detect some meaningful resemblance between what he has come to see in himself and what his sharpened awareness tells him others judge and expect him to be.

In another context, Erikson says that the matter of Identity is established when a young person can answer two questions, "What have I got?" and "What am I going to do with it?" The reader will notice that Identity is not simply the sum of a person's childhood identifications or even the sum of one's childhood. When Erikson speaks of forging an Identity "out of the effective remnants of his childhood," he is speaking of

39

childhood as the material out of which a person creates a self. Youth does not, like God, create out of nothing. My childhood has a lot to do with "what I have got." The word "forge" is an interesting one. You get the picture of a blacksmith with a piece of iron, pounding it with a hammer into a certain shape: a horseshoe, a nail, a ring. The word "forge" indicates that I have a hand in shaping my identity, even if I no longer have a hand in deciding what childhood I had. My childhood is a given; it is over and complete. From it I must choose. From it I must forge a central perspective and some working unity. I am the black-smith of my own Identity.

2. Society and Identity

Please note that I do not form my Identity from my childhood alone; no, I have my hopes for later life, too. I must blend the childhood with the hopes in some workable way. Furthermore, and not surprisingly, I must take into account what my sharpened awareness tells me others judge and expect me to be. And so, the dimension of society. No person, if Erikson is right, can divorce herself from the expectations of society. I may disagree with others; I may react in opposition to what others judge me to be, but the others have an influence whether I like it or not, whether I am aware of their influence or not.

3. How Long it Lasts

Let us go back to a question raised earlier in this discussion of the crisis of Identity, the question of duration. If we make "youth" refer to the time of Identity formation, we can say that youth ends when the crisis of Identity ends. And when is that? I know of no easy answer. Martin Luther's crisis of Identity ended when he emerged as a great preacher at the age of thirty! Gandhi emerged as a reformer at twenty-five. What for us lesser mortals? Erikson does note that the time of Identity crisis for persons of genius is frequently prolonged. He further notes that in our industrial society, identity formation tends to be long, because it takes us so long to gain the skills needed for adulthood's tasks in our technological world. So...we do not have an exact time span in which to find ourselves. It doesn't happen automatically at eighteen or at twenty-one. A very approximate rule of thumb for our society would put the end somewhere in one's twenties.

4. Moratorium

Erikson characterizes this time in life as a time of delay; he uses the Latin word "moratorium."

> This period can be viewed as a psychosocial moratorium during which the young adult through free role experimentation may find a niche in some section of his society, a niche which is firmly defined and yet seems to be uniquely made for him...
>
> A moratorium is a period of delay granted to somebody who is not ready to meet an obligation or forced on somebody who should give himself time. It is a period that is characterized by a selective permissiveness on the part of society and of provocative playfulness on the part of youth, and yet it also often leads to deep, if often transitory, commitments on the part of the youth, and ends in a more or less ceremonial confirmation on the part of society...
>
> Each society and each culture institutionalizes a certain moratorium for the majority of its young people.

And so, we see that the business of "finding one's self" is not a matter of mere study or looking in the mirror. It is a matter of experimentation, or as Erikson puts it, a matter of "free role experimentation." How do I find out what I've got? By trying different things. The whole idea of a period of delay is to give youth the time needed to experiment. Erikson's comment that all societies provide structure for such periods can be seen by such institutions as colleges and universities, the armed forces, the Peace Corps and other organizations like it, to name some common institutions in our own time.

B. Older Outsiders

In any and all of such institutions, there are

adults outside the family framework who work with young people as teachers, counsellors, clergy, drill sergeants and superiors of various kinds.

1. Mentors

Some of these become mentors to youth...as Erikson puts it, "helping the young to overcome unuseable identifications with the parent of the same sex." Mentors are the kind of people who recognize the genius of a given youth and succeed in putting it to work. Frequently, they form a vital part of the resolving the question, the "What have I got?", as well as the question "What am I going to do with it?", both so vital in the resolving of the crisis of Identity.

2. Negative Identity

If older authority figures can become mentors, it is equally true that they can become instrumental in the forming of negative identity. Young people, given provocation, sometimes choose from among their child-hood experiences a perverse identity, based upon roles and persons presented to them as most undesirable or dangerous. Erikson cites as an example a young man who thoroughly lived up to the expectations of a cruel judge who told him in court that he would be in prison within five years.

C. Other Characteristics

1. Creative Tension

At this point, I would like to remind the reader that the stage of Identity carries within it the same tensions expressed in every stage of psychosocial development. This time is marked by the experience of Identity Confusion as well as successfully forging, however briefly, elements of childhood with hopes for adulthood. It is this creative tension that can give birth to a certain central perspective and direction, characterized by the vital strength of fidelity. Erikson sees the period of youth as a time of searching for something worth being faithful to, a message, a way of life, an ethic.

2. Being Faithful (Fidelity)

It matters not if the message is inevitably a

simplistic one. It doesn't matter if the initial formation of a code to live by is much more likely to be negatively put than positively. Most people find out what they are against long before they know what they are for. Erikson's concern is that youth find something to be faithful to. That something, whether it be the message of Christ or the message of Marx, is usually seen as a total message, ruling out all other messages; in short, the first values of youth are generally ideological. No exceptions are allowed; other ways of life are excluded. Erikson benignly expects that the enthusiastic narrowness of youth has the rest of life to find out the exceptions and qualifications to the chosen gospel. His fear is not so much the narrowness of youth as the possibility that no choice, however narrow, will be made at all. He fears an aimless life far more than a way of life that initially smacks of fanaticism.

D. Earlier Stages in New Forms

If the stage of Identity resembles the other stages in its innate creative tension, it resembles the others as well in that each of the preceding stages, although not quite center stage, is alive and in a special way characteristic of youth.

Erikson has been very explicit about how earlier stages (and later stages) surface during the period of Identity Crisis. The reader can turn to the chart in Appendix C to see them in the horizontal line, going left and right, from Stage Five: Identity vs. Identity Confusion.

1. Trust and Time (Temporal Perspective
   vs. Time Confusion)

Thus, there is certainly a crisis of trust in youth, far different from the trust crisis of the new-born, but rooted in the newborn experience of trust. Frequently, young people suffer an agony of trust with the duration of time. Nothing they want comes fast enough; everything takes too long, seemingly forever. Young people ask themselves, "When will I get it together?" It seems to take forever to get out of college or to finish a hitch in the armed services. Time itself becomes hard to trust. There is always the temptation to cut short the precious period of delay granted by society to youth because it is so indefinite, so terribly unsettled. One longs for something clear and finite, someone to hold on to, whether or not solid answers have been formed yet about one's identity. Premature commitments to marriage or career are often attempts to end the hardship of living a life of searching. A premature ending of this period merely puts off to a later date the answers to its questions. Solving identity problems after contracting marriage, having children, or becoming an engineer is a bigger problem than solving those problems earlier in life...for commitments of this nature usually bring the period of delay and leisure to an abrupt halt and often make demands that radically cut the time and the ambience necessary for self discovery in this most basic sense.

2. Autonomy and Certainty (Self-Certainty vs. Self-Consciousness)

The crisis of autonomy is present as well in youth, but in a different way than it was for the toddler. The inevitable introspection of youth, together with the sudden body changes of adolescence, almost always bring about a struggle of certainty and comfort against an agony of self-consciousness with one's new body, awakened sexual drive, and new found capacity to look beneath the surface at one's own intentions and the intentions of others. Self-consciousness is as characteristic of youth as rain is characteristic of April. It is a later form of shame and doubt. On the other hand, what father or mother can forget the absolute assurance of a twenty year old son? The arrogance of youth is legendary. Hence, Erikson's youthful version of Autonomy vs. Shame and Doubt: Self-certainty vs. Self-consciousness.

3. Initiative and Roles (Role Experimentation vs. Role Fixation)

What kind of crisis of initiative does one find in adolescence? It is a reminder that young people don't find themselves by introspection alone. Trying on different hats to find which one fits is vital to a choice in hats. Trying different roles is vital in the process of Identity formation. It is as though there is a real me lurking inside that will only be recognized if I try a variety of ways of acting.

Erikson's telling description of adolescent love speaks to this kind of experimentation. He notes that it is characteristic of adolescent couples to talk

44

interminably; he notes that they will perform sexually if the mores of their group demand it, but that talking remains paramount. What are they up to? Recognition, understanding, a hope that in conversation with boyfriend or girlfriend they will find out what they themselves are like. It is like looking in a sympathetic mirror. Hence the hours on the telephone, late talk into the night at parties, and the peculiar and touching dependence that so often characterizes couples of this time in life. They are finding out who they are from each other.

What is the downside of initiative? The counter-player to role experimentation? It is the deadly fix on a single way of acting, cemented in place by a paralyzing fear that another way might lead to disaster, embarrassment, or evil. I choose one way of acting because it is seemingly safe and I don't feel guilty if I stick with it. Whether or not it fits is not the point. Picture a student in an engineering program because that's what Dad wants. Period. That's it. Picture a young woman studying to be a teacher, because that's what girls do. Period. That's it. Picture a promiscuous young athlete, because that is how jocks act. Period. And so the battleground between safety and experiment, always in search of one's true self...or for a mixture of old identifications that somehow fits.

4.   Industry and Apprenticeship
      (Apprenticeship vs. Work Paralysis)

If the primary school years focused on learning the skills necessary for adulthood, the years of high school, and later apprenticeships (more and more typically found in college today), have a similar but more sophisticated demand for a competency in adult skills. Erikson calls this older version of Industry vs. Inferiority, Apprenticeship vs. Work Paralysis.

What college student has not gone through dead periods when work seemed impossible? It is a truism that somewhere along the line an undergraduate has a semester characterized by sleeping, partying, tremendous bouts of eating, or just staying in the room doing nothing--anything to avoid doing the required work. And yet, a successful apprenticeship, whether in college or elsewhere, demands enthusiasm and hard work. In later years, there is always the memory of a favorite course, a professor who took me

under her wing, a program...that feeling of apprenticeship...being a beginner and loving it; being on my
own, with no guarantee that I will do well or even
finish, but with a joyous determination to give it my
all, no matter what the results, no matter what the
cost in terms of time, energy or money. We are talking
about the enthusiasm of the novice learner, whether in
a trade, preparing for a profession, or beginning a
line of work.

Of course, real life is a tension between two
extremes, experiencing now the joy of working, now the
paralysis that goes with boredom and lack of
commitment.

E. Later Stages Anticipated

With this treatment of the world of work comes
the end of a treatment of updated versions of past
crises.

1. Youth as a Bridge

We have noted that the process of identity
formation is made not only from the effective remnants
of my childhood, but also in the hopes of my anticipated adulthood. If the past is important, so is the
future. There is lots of dreaming about, and planning
for, the future in adolescence. In Erikson's description of the life cycle, there are three stages that
occur after the crisis of Identity. Each one of these
is typically anticipated in adolescence.

Since we have not yet taken the later stages, it
is the plan of this book to interrupt the present
treatment of youth. We will take a good hard look at
the stages coming later, and then come back to finish
the treatment of Youth.

The reason is simple. Erikson is quite clear that
each one of his stages has earlier forms as well as
later ones. True, there is a time in life when each
stage has center stage, so to speak. Again, we refer
the reader to the chart in Appendix C.

2. Central Perspective

What is unique about the stage of Identity is
that it is a special sort of synthesis of earlier
stages and a special sort of anticipation of later

46

ones. Youth has a certain unique quality in a person's life; it is a bridge between childhood and adulthood. Youth is a time of radical change--the great body changes accompanying puberty, the ability of the mind to search one's own intentions and the intentions of others, the suddenly sharpened awareness of the roles society has offered for later life. Remembering the words of Erikson once more...that youth...

> must forge...some central perspective and direction, some working unity, out of the effective remnants of his childhood and the hopes of his anticipated adulthood; he must detect some meaningful resemblance between what he has come to see in himself and what his sharpened awareness tells him others judge and expect him to be.

In this context, the words "central perspective and direction, some working unity" are most important. They emphasize the period of Identity as a central crossroad in life. There will be other crossroads, other crises, yet this one has a certain centrality; it will leave an indelible mark on adulthood just as it sums up all of childhood. It is a time of choice par excellence.

That is the reason that Erikson spells out so carefully the updated forms of each childhood crisis, and why he shows the specific anticipatory look at the adult crises to come.

In order to be able to understand how the later stages are anticipated, we present them now, halfway through the treatment of Identity. When we have shown them all, we will return to the subject of Identity with a good grasp of the stages that follow it.

RECOMMENDED READINGS FOR CHAPTER THREE

Which of Erikson's work does this chapter suggest? There is an excellent, short description of adolescence in Childhood and Society, Chapter Seven. Erikson's essay on the youth of Adolph Hitler in Chapter Nine is also apropos. Young Man Luther, as has been noted, is essentially the biography of an adolescent. It is a brilliant book.

For a description of how each stage in the life cycle is present in adolescence, see Identity: Youth and Crisis, Chapter IV, Part 4, I. This entire book is devoted to youth; most of it is not easy going.

As for pictures of the Crisis of Identity in the world of literature, let us note first, Shakespeare's Hamlet, Prince of Denmark. Erikson himself comments on this great play in Chapter Seven of Identity: Youth and Crisis. Romeo and Juliet is certainly a play about adolescent love, if Shakespeare is to your taste.

J. D. Salinger's The Catcher in the Rye and Sylvia Plath's The Bell Jar are two modern novels which startlingly reveal the crisis of youth.

The world of film is another powerful witness. I recommend The Graduate, Dustin Hoffman's classic portrayal of a young man in the sixties. More recently: Breaking Away, The Diner, Gregory's Girl. I have not found movies of quality on this crisis in the lives of young women.

For the reader who is interested in the whole notion of mentors for youth, so vital to an understanding of the Crisis of Identity, I recommend first Erikson's references to Dr. Staupitz in Young Man Luther. Daniel Levinson and his associates have enlarged on the notion of mentors for young men in The Seasons of a Man's Life. We await a forthcoming volume from Levinson and company on women's development and the treatment of mentors for women which he is currently researching.

CHAPTER IV

ADULTHOOD (STAGES SIX AND SEVEN)

If we are to leave the stage of Identity and youth in the middle, having seen how each childhood stage reemerges in a new form to be fashioned, one hopes, into some effective new unity, it is a good place to stop. For, as we have seen, the fashioning of an Identity concerns not only the effective remnants of one's childhood, it looks to the future as well. There is an anticipation of what is to come. It seems good sense then, in this treatment, to move on, with the stage of Identity only half done, and to look how Erikson describes the stages to come. Then we will have a better vantage point to pick up once again the formation of Identity, this time looking to the future stages as well as the past. The future stages then. In adulthood there are two of them. The first, following immediately upon the formation of Identity, is a crisis of Intimacy.

A. Intimacy vs. Isolation

1. Intimacy and Identity

Mature intimacy can only occur in the light of an established Identity. Or so says our theorist. During the years of the Identity crisis my intimates are generally people who help me find out about myself. There is an intimacy, all right, but it is centered on the self rather than the other person. Once a sort of working unity is established, I can afford to establish intimate relationships more concerned with the other person. Nor will I have to contend to as great a degree with the fear that my intimates will somehow swallow me up if I have a working grasp of what I have and the general direction I want to go.

This established working unity enables those whom I seek as friends to have something in me to count on, a certain settled quality. It is this being at home with myself that is the rock on which one can build enduring adult relationships. The most obvious example is marriage, but it is important to see that personal commitments of an enduring nature are not always found within the marriage bond. Sometimes, the commitments are never formalized by ceremony. There are commitments to live a celibate life in common for some higher goal. There are long friendships now

49

involving marriage. Mature friendship is built on the
same foundation as marriage.

2. Isolation

The   concern   for close friendship is the heart of
this stage. Its counterquality is Isolation. I hasten
to add that isolation can occur at the heart of a
partnership,   when   seeming   friends conspire to keep a
potentially deep involvement on the surface. The term
isolation does not mean just physical isolation, like
living alone in the woods. It more frequently occurs
in crowds; it is a shadow in the lives of lovers who
are physically together but not sharing one with the
other whatever is there in the deeper self. Isolation
is a mask, a front, an arm outstretched to keep friends
from coming too close.

What intimates have not had to contend with a wall
of isolation somehow arising between them? It is precisely the existence of such walls and our efforts to
pierce them that forms the dynamic tension of this time
in life.   Intimacy and Isolation are Siamese twins;
where you have one, you have the other.

3. Emerging Strength: Love

The emerging vital strength to be hoped for is,
simply, love...a love between equals, in which I can
hope to give myself to someone else without being
terrified that I myself will disappear. It is a love
characterized by a genuine mutuality and the basic
maintenance of each person's self.   This is not a
servant-master relationship; it is more a matter of
mutual help and mutual enhancement. More than anything else, it is a love that is willing to put up
with times of isolation, informed as it is, by
childhood's trust and hope.

4. Societal Variations

What sort of societal variations do you find for
this crisis? I note for the benefit of the reader
that Erikson's treatment of Intimacy is downright
sparse in comparison with what he has to say of other
stages.   There are indications, however, that the
stage of Intimacy is sometimes merged with the stage
before it or the one after. Martin Luther moved very
quickly to marriage after he "found his voice."   He
went from monastery to wedding bed very quickly. In

Luther, the crisis of intimacy and the crisis of generativity occurred at the same time. The lonely and sorrowful monk soon learned intimacy within the marriage bond. It is worth noting that Luther's long history of friendships with men began at this time as well. Intimacy is not restricted, in Erikson's scheme of things, to sexual intimacies, but to the entire range of friendship.

Erikson notes in another context that women in our society frequently fuse the crisis of Identity with that of Intimacy. He speaks of the formation of a woman's Identity when she welcomes a man into her own inner "space." However, he seems, to this writer, to have taken seriously in his later years the occupational changes in contemporary women. Many of them have careers before marriage; many have grown up in a home where their own mothers had outside jobs. The implication is that the career or work aspect of the Identity of many modern women has shifted to sharing of home responsibility with a partner and a career outside the home. Thus Erikson's wife Joan, to whom he refers frequently in his later years as a coauthor with him in all his writings, puts the matter bluntly:

> Don't you think that nowadays, particularly for young women, the idea of the need for a separate identity starts much earlier in girls' minds and they're not going to wait until they get married? Right now it seems to me that in many parts of society it's become quite clear that women have got to start thinking early about what they can do and who they are...a lot of women are just not going to get married if they don't find a partner who will cooperate in letting them develop their long-range capacities and work interests.

Joan Erikson reminds us that there is a societal dimension to every stage in her husband's eight stages; and this includes both Identity and Intimacy. It seems clear that societal factors today cause many women to find their own Identities quite apart from the experience of Intimacy with a prospective mate.

Carol Gilligan, a contemporary developmentalist, comments on the validity of Erikson's stages for women. She praises Erikson for noting that women often fuse Identity with Intimacy concerns. She notes that most women choose careers with a concern for people as very important to their choices. Such a concern generally comes at a later time for men. Hence the basic validity of Erikson's initial observation that women often fuse Identity concerns with Intimacy concerns. Gilligan is not commenting so much on a woman's choice of mate as vital to her Identity as her concern for the people with whom she will work in a given career.

She takes Erikson to task for not pursuing this basic insight of his further. His fullest descriptions of the Crisis of Identity all concern men.

I have myself noted that Erikson has little to say about Intimacy as a stage in his biography of Mohandas Gandhi. Gandhi was married when he was thirteen years old, according to the Hindu custom of his day. His experiences of marital intimacy seem diffused through a number of stages. I find it interesting that the marriage customs of his time and country blur a well marked stage of Intimacy following the time of Identity. Gandhi was a perfectly respectable father before he knew his own Identity. Granted that it was a fatherhood within an extended family that could do very nicely with children of fathers and mothers who themselves were not much more than children. Gandhi's own mother was very much the mother of his children, while he and his wife Kasturbai were growing up themselves. Perhaps one could make a case for keeping Identity, Intimacy, and Generativity rather separate despite different societal circumstances; but my point here is that Erikson himself seems content to let the lines blur. It would seem that Gandhi slowly learned intimacy during his marriage, as he slowly came to know himself during his marriage, and that he slowly learned generativity during his marriage, his Intimacy time and his Identity time. The lines of separation between these stages, for societal reasons as well as a personal history of wide travelling when he was a very young man, have conspired to make temporal distinctions in these three stages difficult in the life of this remarkable man. The case of modern woman, and the biographies of both Luther and Gandhi certainly underline the societal influence on just how the stage of Intimacy vs. Isolation occurs.

Perhaps in closing the societal aspects of this stage, we should mention a conviction on the part of Erikson that intimacy and sexual promiscuity don't have much to do with each other. With the advent of sexual freedom, where both men and women can separate having sex from having kids, has come a kind of neofrigidity, the ability to make love without love. People have had "intimacies" without Intimacy in most times of the world's history, but it is easier in some times than in others. And so, being able "to get it on" is not an indicator of the kind of commitment which Erikson demands for Intimacy; it can be a mockery of Intimacy; it can be the hallmark of the predatory wolflike individual, for whom commitment is not even a consideration. Contemporary woman's rejection of the predatory male is built precisely upon her rage at being used without commitment by a man, especially if the male in question used the lover's words of commitment without any intention of having them carry any farther than the covers of a bed. Lists of promiscuous "intimacies", no matter how long, don't add up to Intimacy; generally, they are classic examples of Isolation.

5.   Reappearance in Later Life

Moving on, then, to the reappearance of this crisis in later stages of life. How does it appear? The most memorable of Erikson's own examples is his use of the character of an old man in Ingmar Bergman's classic film, Wild Strawberries. Erikson points out that the old man in the story, a famous physician, had failed to win the sweetheart of his youth. His intellectual cast of mind and his inability to show his feelings for her caused him to lose her, and at the same time, sowed the seeds of a cold and frigid marriage to another woman in later life. In old age, he experienced a sort of proud and bitter isolation, the accumulation of the years come home to haunt him. His refusal to help in the marriage of his son, so much like his own failed marriage, shows clearly both his despairing isolation as well as his having handed his own aloofness on to his own son.

The story in the film shows how his daughter-in-law manages to break through the old man's thick shell to find, buried deep, a heart still alive. She enlists his aid and concern, so long dormant, in her own effort to crack through the all too familiar distance and reserve of her own husband, breaking a

53

pattern of isolation passed on for generations in her husband's family.

The unresolved crisis of Intimacy in the old man is partly resolved in his old age, even though his wife is long dead and his own life is nearing its end. The son of the old Doctor, in his prime years, has clearly also not resolved a similar crisis. His inability to show love for his own wife, his repugnance to having children of his own, and the bitterness of his own isolation in the married state--all these are forms of earlier isolation. It is worthwhile saying as well, that his own wife's successful effort, with help from his father, to reclaim him from an emotional scrap pile, are evidence that there was indeed some remnant left from his youth, some spark from days gone by, which she was able to kindle to a small flame...enough for her, and containing within itself the possibility of greater warmth.

Clearly, the crisis of intimacy has forms in the later stages of human life. How interesting that Erikson himself used this film in teaching his own system to undergraduate students at Harvard during the decade of the nineteen sixties. As he once said, "A system needs a good story."

6. Having it Made?

In closing this description, I would add that there is no such thing as "having it made" in this description. Erik Erikson's stages have no niches where effort and struggle are no longer needed. In this particular stage, his position is stark and blunt, "There is no intimacy without the experience of isolation. There is no intimacy without the risk of permanent isolation." Intimacy always involves taking a chance. It always involves making a commitment. And if one learns to love another or others, then what? Then there is a new emphasis gradually forthcoming, a new center of concern. Then begins the crisis of Generativity.

B. Generativity vs. Stagnation

1. Generativity

This is the longest of all the stages in the lives of most people. It encompasses the middle years of the life cycle. It could last twenty, thirty, or

54

even forty years. It is more the age of parents than the age of grandparents, more the age of mothering and fathering than the age of establishing a loving relationship. One need not be a marriage partner, of course, or a parent. But to be a father in some sense, a mother in some sense, that is a requisite. If mothers and fathers generally take it upon themselves to generate children and to care for them, people in these middle years are seen by Erikson as needing in some way to care for the generation coming up under them. There are a thousand ways of being a father other than being a biological parent and an equal number of ways for being a mother.

Erikson is quick to point out that our own times demand what might be called a "care for the children of the world" far more than they ask for us to produce children of our own. He feels that in a time of planned parenthood, including the planning to have no children, that there is a quality of what he calls "procreativity" deep in human nature that must be exercised for one to be an ethical person. He means that middle aged people must somehow help shoulder the burden of the children of the world. Not to do so, whether one is a parent or not, leads to what he calls "Stagnation."

2. Stagnation

The word "stagnant" carries with it an image of decay, of rotting. A stagnant pond has a bad smell. So does a stagnant person. In a withering description of stagnation in a person of mature years, Erikson says that a person whose life is stagnant seems to treat himself as though he himself were his own children. There is a quality of self-centeredness, sometimes demanding total order in a home, obsessed with the small details of living. Frequently, there is a gnawing overconcern with one's health. Think of a woman whose makeup is never smeared, whose house is never messy, who is dominated by the latest health fad, the new doctor in town, the exact right amount of vitamins per meal. Think of a man who can't stand being called at the office, who erupts if he doesn't see every play of a televised football game, who is either always impeccably dressed or always embarrassingly shabby and slovenly, whose routine is either totally rigid, or who has no routine at all.

In any case, regardless of detail, we are talking

about a middle aged person whose sun rises and sets on himself. If the reader is of this age and feels a bit queasy at finding something of his own life here, then it is again time to remind that reader that there is no Generativity without the experience of Stagnation. No one who is a caring person has emerged with that vital strength without periods of Stagnation. The battle between these two enemies is never over; nor could one exist without the other.

In one of his later works, Erikson mentions that he realized in his own middle years how frequently the quality of Stagnation is marked by a terrible and punitive anger. A person not only does not want to be helpful to partner and children, but there is an urge to put them down, to punish out of proportion, and to make children and family into scapegoats. This attitude is often extended to people outside the family, especially towards persons, peoples, and nations seen as outsiders.

3. Later Comments

If he has expanded in his later work on the characteristics of Stagnation, he has also discussed in greater detail the good wood of maturity. He finds a certain creative quality, not necessarily tied to the procreation of children, but embracing the world of ideas, and the world of work. Generativity is often expressed in productivity of many kinds. This creative, generative, productive aspect of the mature character is frequently marked by a certain child-likeness. There is a certain knowing naivety, a kind of playfulness in the creative and productive character. He has noticed this playful creativeness in the mature years of such diverse characters as Einstein and Gandhi. He has seen it in the tremendous literary productivity of George Bernard Shaw and Martin Luther. He has seen it in the work ethic of the American father. We have tantalizing comments about Golda Meir's political imagination, "Golda was quite a momma," says Erikson. He admits to being fascinated as well with the sixteenth century Carmelite nun, Teresa of Avila, whose imagination and leadership among women of her own time caused him to be tempted to try a biography. All these diverse people had their mature years characterized by great productivity and frequently by amazingly different ways of caring for other people.

4. Societal Aspects

If we are to deal directly with the societal aspects of the generative years, two historical figures emerge in the writings of Erik Erikson meriting special notice. They are Mohandas Gandhi and Thomas Jefferson. A brief description of their differences may here illustrate societal factors at work in their generative years.

Erikson's treatment of Gandhi has Gandhi's generative years as its special object. Gandhi, the Father of modern India, expressed his parenthood in a way peculiarly Indian. The traditional Hindu and Jain reverence for life was brought by Gandhi from private and religious life to the public arena, the political sphere, and used as a weapon to free India from the domination of Great Britain. It is precisely this caring attitude in Gandhi that concerns Erikson. It is as though Gandhi acted as parent to both the people of India and the occupying British as well, evidenced by his refusal to espouse violence as a means of removing the Occupier. He refused to hate the English forces either; his insistence on respect for the adversary, while still regarding him as an adversary, is seen by Erikson as caring, the virtue characteristic of fathers and mothers. Gandhi possessed a kind of blatant maternalism, that found him in the role of nurse not only in his family and ashram, but in prisons, too; in fact, toward anyone he came in contact with, friend or enemy. Erikson finds him an amazingly maternal person, concerned as he was with peace, right at the core of his effort to oust the English overlords.

It was as though peace itself were a weapon, as though respect for an enemy could conquer the enemy, as though powerlessness and refusal to hate is the greatest weapon of all. Such a political use of nonviolence has its roots in Hindu religion and is anchored in Hindu society. Gandhi's use of it remains unique, it is true. No Indian had ever used nonviolence for political means before him. Yet no one but an Indian was likely to have discovered this very practical usage. Gandhi was a very Indian politician and a very caring, mother-and-father-like statesman. Erikson sees him as a prophetic figure for the politicians of the future if the world is to survive this nuclear age.

Thomas Jefferson, although not given the same attention by Erikson as to merit a full-length biography, nevertheless has attracted Erikson as a generative person. Jefferson's middle years found him not only as author of the Declaration of Independence, President of the United States, householder in Virginia, in fact in a bewildering variety of occupations--architect, surveyor, litterateur, inventor, farmer, philosopher, and teacher. He wrote a still extant commentary on the Gospels. His very ingenuity and flexibility made him a peculiar American prototype, expressing at one time the ingenuity of the American entrepreneur, yet at the same time, not becoming so pragmatic and flexible as to lose any sense of ethics. Erikson sees a kind of unbridled flexibility as haunting the American Dream, lacking in any guiding sense of what is right and wrong, so intent is it on fitting in or making a dollar.

Jefferson's passionate concern for individual rights, for the rising of a natural aristocracy of merit rather than the European model of an aristocracy of birth, gives evidence of his care for the individual person and his rights. If his libertarian views, so radical for his time, seem flawed to modern eyes by his reluctant espousal of slavery as well as an eye that did not grant participation in government and the world of commerce to women, these very faults underline the breadth of his vision for his own day.

He was a very caring President, he was a very caring father, fulfilling as best he could the roles of both mother and father to his children upon his wife's early death. Despite his warlike attitude toward the English, in such contrast to Gandhi's attitude a hundred years later toward the same English oppressor, there was, nevertheless, in the man Jefferson an unusually maternal strain. His attitude towards his children, as well as his attention to the smallest details of householding bear witness to this. Erikson has noted the great maternal cupolas over his home at Monticello as well as at the University of Virginia, both of which were carefully chosen by Jefferson himself. No Washington monument for him! This creative man, seen as embodying to remarkable lengths, both maternal and paternal qualities in the sphere of politics and home, is depicted by Erikson as embodying much of the caring qualities that characterize the strength of life's middle years. His concern for the brutalizing effects of the institution of slavery on children, both black and white, sounds a prophetic note in today's America. His desire for equality, however flawed, is peculiar to the best in the American spirit; his inventiveness and flexibility, his belief in an aristocracy of merit is American, too; rooted in the desire for freedom handed on by the colonists who came before him. He is seen by Erikson as a very American father, a very American politician, a person whose caring in both politics and home are as American in origin as Gandhi's militant nonviolence is Indian.

5. Other Forms in Other Stages

And so, a glimpse at two quite different kinds of generativity. It is a time to look for just how this great middle period of the life cycle might manifest itself in later years. Now that we are down at the end of the cycle, there is only one stage to come, the stage of old age, the last. Old age concerns itself with coming to terms with a person's one and only life cycle. There will be no second chance; its question: "Can I live with a life already lived? Or do I despair of it, now that things are coming down to the wire?"

Erikson speaks of "grand" generativity for old people, a detached concern for sons and daughters who themselves are parents, as well as for the children of those sons and daughters. Grandmothers and grand-fathers frequently have "adopted" children and grandchildren. The special quality of being detached, living a time of life when one knows that one will have to let go: this lends itself to a special quality of wisdom which can be more objective than the caring of parents. Of course, "grandgenerativity" is made difficult today, because of the dispersed quality of the family. There can be, as well, a continuing sense of stagnation, left over from another stage, a sense of mourning for opportunities lost, children uncared for, intimacy missed.

Here the figure of Dr. Borg in the film already alluded to, Wild Strawberries, comes to the fore once again. His initial refusal, in the proud isolation of his old age, to be of any help to his daughter-in-law, who has come to him to seek his wisdom. He will have none of her problem...and yet through a series of dreams and incidents on a motor trip--above all because of the tenacity and bluntness of his daughter-in-law he manages to renegotiate a middle age, marked by a loveless marriage. He does this by showing concern for another woman, his son's wife; strangely succeeding, he shows love for a woman for the first time in his life, a father's love, which he had denied his own son. His disdain and remoteness melted at last. If he failed a test of intimacy as a young man and later as a husband, if he also failed as a parent to care for his son, he is given a sort of final reprieve, whereby he can succeed at last as a "grand" old man--showing at the end the kind of concern for a son's marriage that he never showed for his own.

At this point, it seems good to remind the reader that if the stage of generativity is present in a "grand" way in old age, it is present as well by way of anticipation in earlier stages. It should be no surprise that Gandhi, whose care for others as a mature man was marked by a habitual playfulness, should have developed this quality as a child during the stage of Initiative vs. Guilt. He was a playful and teasing little boy; as a man, he teased the British Lion with a gentle tenacity that caused that lion mighty discomfort and eventual departure. The little boy Moniya was very much alive in the great holy man, Mahatma Gandhi. That his early teasing should much later take the form of militant gadfly who refused to be lured into violence or hatred, showing care and concern for British forces occupying his country, but at the same time needling them unmercifully... this is evidence that a person's past lives on in later life in a new way. The crisis of generativity lives on, then, in old age, and it is anticipated in all the stages that go before it.

This ends our treatment of the middle years; now for the end, the last stage, termed by Erikson the crisis of Integrity.

READINGS SUGGESTED BY THIS CHAPTER

For those readers who are reading Childhood and Society, there are excellent descriptions of Intimacy/Isolation and Generativity/Stagnation in Chapter Seven.

Gandhi's Truth is a biography centering on Gandhi's middle years, but by no means neglecting how his early years gave birth to his peculiar and motherly fatherhood of India, summed up in his now famous militant nonviolence.

Dimensions of a New Identity is a very short book about Thomas Jefferson's middle years and the need of contemporary Americans to see him as embodying much of the best of a mature American morality. Likely an easier book to tackle than Gandhi's Truth. Another book, Adulthood, is edited by Erikson and contains a chapter by him on the character, Dr. Borg, in Ingmar Bergman's film, Wild Strawberries. I find this chapter to be the finest short statement I have read on three of Erikson's stages, Intimacy/Isolation, Generativity/ Stagnation, and its focal point, the time of old age.

Joan Erikson's remarks on intimacy are taken from The Harvard Educational Review, Number Two, Volume fifty-one. Erikson's remarks on Golda Meir and Teresa of Avila are also in this issue of The Harvard Educational Review.

As for excursions into the world of literature, I would remind the reader that Erikson has never written a biography of a woman. This has not gone unnoticed by his critics. If he has indicated that women frequently tie Intimacy and Identity together into one stage, it has been left to other authors to elaborate on this. Among the more eloquent and certainly among the more literary of these is Carol Gilligan. Read Chapter One, "A Woman's Place in a Man's Life Cycle," and Chapter Four, "Crisis and Transition," from In a Different Voice by Carol Gilligan.

The novels of Identity Crisis among women become all the more important in the absence of a biography by Erikson. Sylvia Plath's Bell Jar will give the reader a picture of a young woman struggling with both Identity and Intimacy issues. Robertson Davies provides another really brilliant novel of Intimacy/Identity in his story of a young singer,

<u>A Mixture of Frailties</u>. Margaret Laurence writes
beautifully of the struggle against isolation in all of
her novels. I recommend especially <u>The Diviners</u> and
<u>A Jest of God</u>. The latter has an excellent film
version, starring Joanne Woodward, <u>Rachel, Rachel</u>.

Intimacy, of course, is the poet's special
corner; pick your own. My favorites: the sonnets of
Shakespeare and the poems of e.e. cummings.

There are many novelists of the dark side of
generativity: John Updike's <u>Rabbit</u> trilogy and Graham
Greene's novels, especially <u>The Heart of the Matter</u>.
Bernard Malamud writes somber stories of the struggle
for generativity. <u>The Fixer</u> and his most recent,
<u>God's Grace</u>, come to mind. Walker Percy's <u>The Second</u>
<u>Coming</u>. And, of course, we cannot leave out
Shakespeare's plays--<u>MacBeth</u>, <u>Julius Caesar</u>, and
<u>Othello</u>--all plays in which the generative side of
mature adults is swallowed up in the dark shadow of
what Erikson calls "Stagnation."

It is harder to find examples in literature where
the positive side of the pull between generativity and
stagnation predominates. For the most part, healthy
adults don't make good drama. Still, I suggest Graham
Greene's <u>Monsignor Quixote</u> and again, Margaret
Laurence's <u>The Diviners</u>.

CHAPTER V

OLD AGE (STAGE EIGHT): INTEGRITY VS. DESPAIR

A. Integrity

We had better begin with the meaning of the word
"integrity." It is not an easy word to get hold of.
In common usage, integrity often means honesty, as in
the phrase, "a person of integrity." Erikson doesn't
quite mean that; his meaning is closer to the Latin
root of the word, which indicates "wholeness" or "being
all in one piece." Webster says, "a quality or state
of being complete or undivided." COMPLETENESS is a
synonym. So Erikson himself speaks of integrity as a
sense of coherence and wholeness, noting that such a
sense is in the face of loss of connectedness--the
body's circulatory system is weaker; musculature loses
tone and strength. The mind is losing its ability to
remember. The surrounding community frequently
threatens the older person with a loss of responsible
function in the interplay between the generations.
In the face of these forces of division and decay,
then, arises the need for a sense of "holding things
together."

At the end of a life lived, of course, there is a
priceless opportunity to "put things together" in a way
never possible before. After all, there is only one
time in life when you have lived a whole life, and that
is at the end. Binding together the experiences of a
lifetime is the task of old age, and old age is the
only time in life affording an opportunity to do so.
The task involved is the acceptance of the life that
has, as a matter of fact, been mine and nobody else's.
Let Erikson speak for himself:

> The acceptance of one's one and only
> life cycle as something that had to
> be and that by necessity permitted of
> no substitutions. Although aware of
> the relativity of the various life
> styles which have given meaning to
> human striving, the possessor of
> integrity is ready to defend the
> dignity of his own life style against
> all physical and economic threats.

B. Despair

And what of Integrity's counterquality, Despair?
The word despair, in its root, means "without hope." It
expresses the feeling that the time is now short, too
short for attempting another life. I'm simply stuck
with most of it; for most of it is already lived.
Erikson speaks of old people as mourning the lost
opportunities of the past. "Perhaps I should have
stayed there." "Perhaps I should have done this...or
that." He speaks of the "thousand little disgusts" of
old age, not the least of which are the continuing
small losses of memory, body strength, and responsible
function. A quote from an aunt of mine, vigorous
still, about the coming of old age..."and then when
you're older you get sick, oh dear!"

And yet, Erikson, writing in his own old age,
notes that without the experience of despair there is
no chance to get an integrated sense of one's life.
The downside part of every stage is a part of life.
To be able to have a hopeful sense of the whole of it
must include the failures. The failures live on in
seducing memories, carrying the old person to queru-
lousness and indecision, to the bitter disdain of the
days left, to an overwhelming disgust at the forces of
decay always present, always reminding one of lost
vigor.

C. Emerging Strength

And what does Erikson see as the emerging strength
of this struggle between Integrity and Despair? He
speaks of Wisdom, and defines it as "a kind of informed
and detached concern with life in the face of death
itself."

And if Wisdom is the strength to be hoped for,
does it take different forms in different societies?
In a recent interview as well as in his last book,
Erikson speaks of the old person as once having been
one of the few survivors; not many people live to see
old age in much of the world. And yet in America
today, in the era of modern medicine, we have whole
colonies of what he calls not "elders" but "elderlies."
The once few dispensers of wisdom have become a crowd,
not so special as they once were, but having the power
of numbers. There is an obvious danger to the revered
status of old age if it becomes a commonplace...and in
the United States it has. Americans do not look for

wisdom in their old people; they send them all to
Florida...and the intergenerational give and take, so
necessary for vital old age, is endangered.

D. Shaw and Gandhi

A contrast in pictures of old age can be drawn
from a comparison of George Bernard Shaw as an old man
with the old man Gandhi. Shaw, in his old age,
described in brilliant detail how he emerged from
obscurity to become the great critic, playwright and
observer of the times of the England of the first three
decades of the twentieth century. There is an unmis-
takable tone of disgust in the description of his youth
written by the now famous G.B.S., looking back on the
tricks and ploys he used to gain notoriety and then
respectability...as if the old man Shaw is not
impressed with the conniving and ambitious youth he
once was. He knows full well that those same qualities
are alive and well in the old man...and there is no
chance to make them any different.

Erikson gives us a brief picture of Gandhi's last
days in India, an old man in his seventies wandering
the streets of Calcutta and other great Indian cities
amid the riots and near warfare that characterized the
division between Moslems and Hindus prior to the
partition of India into a Moslem state and a Hindu
state. His dream of a united India was in ruins; his
message of peace seemed lost; nonviolence only a
memory. Erikson likens him to King Lear wandering
"among the storms and ruins of communal riots which
seemed to mark an end to any hope of a unified India."

And so we see the faint disgust of the famous
Irish man of letters, described in a comfortable old
age, a sort of walking literary shrine attended by
all, but cursed with his own critic's eye; seeing
quite clearly some of his own shallowness. And in
contrast, the man who made a political movement out of
having nothing but an indomitable spirit, rejected by
the very people who once followed his slight figure,
seeing the destruction of his own dream firsthand, in
the streets, alone. It is true, there is a contrast
between these two forms of the dark side of old age,
and yet for this writer there is a reminder that old
age is a time of being stripped...and that people at
the end frequently seem very much more like each other
than they did at any time since they came naked into
the world. So, at the end they will leave it.

E. Other Forms in Other Stages

And do we find forerunners of old age in all the
stages that precede it? The ego's task, we are told,
in every age, is to integrate. The newborn infant
must try to fashion "hope", a virtue of integration,
out of its experience of trust and mistrust...a hope
that, in old age, is called by Erikson "faith." Each
of the stages carries with it a task of integration of
two primary opposing tendencies and of a host of lesser
ones. Each stage demands the integration of what has
gone before with what is now. Each stage must come to
terms with the moment in history in which the person
finds himself.

F. The Final INTEGRITY

Integrity, the making of a totality, a unified
person, from all these diverse elements is always
life's great task. If life's last stage is termed
Integrity vs. Despair, if Integrity is spelled here
with a capital "I", it is because the very end of life
has a whole lifetime to put together, and not just a
part. All the integrations of the past somehow become
part of the final one, the last one, the only one not
followed by another. If there is cause for hope in old
age, it is the hope of mature faith, that dares to
venture a glimpse through a dark glass, that there will
be something else after death.

READINGS SUGGESTED BY THIS CHAPTER

As always, there is a good reference in Childhood and Society. I refer the reader to the famous Chapter Seven of that book.

The interview referred to in this chapter is in Psychology Today, June, 1983. It is accompanied by a stunning series of photograph-portraits of Erikson in full color, as he is today. The reference to George Bernard Shaw is in Identity: Youth and Crisis, Chapter Four.

The most complete treatment of old age in Erikson's work is quite reasonably in his most recent book, The Life Cycle Completed, Chapter Three. Here he reviews the entire eight stages of the life cycle, beginning with the last one, from the perspective of his own old age.

And yet...the gem shining brightest in all his writings on old age remains the brilliant review of Bergman's Wild Strawberries in the first chapter of Adulthood.

Literary treatments of old age are not large in number in this author's adventures in reading, but there are some real jewels. Shakespeare's King Lear must have pride of place. Among modern authors, May Sarton (Kinds of Love) and Margaret Laurence (The Stone Angel) are outstanding.

My favorite film on old age remains Ingmar Bergman's Wild Strawberries. More recently, Harry and Tonto and On Golden Pond are worth mentioning.

CHAPTER VI

YOUTH (STAGE FIVE), <u>CONTINUED</u>

We have now treated the three stages following the establishment of Identity. It is time to return to our treatment of Youth, in order to see how youth anticipates the crises of Intimacy, Generativity, and Integrity.

A. Anticipating Intimacy/Isolation

1. Sexual Polarization vs. Bisexual Confusion

How does youth prepare for the focus on Intimacy that is to come? What form does this preparation take? Erikson speaks of a certain "Sexual Polarization" as characteristic of this stage. Webster defines "polarization" as "division into two groups of opposites." Our author speaks of sexual polarization as a clear settling upon one's sexuality and one's sexual style. The two opposites referred to by Webster are male and female. It is the answer to the question, "What kind of sexual animal am I, given the fact of my maleness or my femaleness?"

Perhaps this polarization can best be understood by its counterquality, called by Erikson, "Bisexual Confusion." It is a common occurrence among adolescents to have confusion about their own sexuality. "Am I gay or straight? How do I know? Whom should I ask?" The stark division between homosexual and heterosexual is only one question about one's sexuality to be asked, one among many. The styles of being a man or woman allow leeway between the polar opposites of homo-and heterosexual.

2. Societal Aspects

There are a lot of different ways of being a man and an increasingly large number of options for being a woman. When women's roles change, men's change, too, the sexes being bound so closely together. In any event, each person has a definite style of sexuality. For men and women this is normally settled before Intimacy is possible. As we have seen, women frequently experience the two crises of Identity and Intimacy at the same time. This added dimension makes the crisis of Identity for most women a more complex time than it is for men, laden as it is with choices not only of career and work, but also with the importance of the people associated with that career--husbands, coworkers, clients and competitors. Put in other terms, women frequently mature more quickly than their male peers when it comes to friends and relationships. I am tempted to say that you don't have to be a social scientist to know that, just an observant person!

Intimacy frequently founders when one simply has established no pattern that one's friend or friends can count on in a life together. If a husband cannot make up his mind, even after marriage, to play the field or to stick to one, his partner could be justly outraged, to cite one example.

3. The Struggle Within

And so, back to the struggle within a single individual between a definite and predictable sexual style versus the isolation and loneliness that inevitably follow from a chameleon like approach to one's own sexuality which not only causes personal confusion, but causes potential intimates to stay at a distance.

B. Anticipating Generativity/Stagnation

1. Following the crisis of Intimacy in Erikson's eight stage life cycle comes the second to last stage. As we have seen, it is normally the longest in time of all of the eight, for it encompasses the entire span of an adult's middle years, right up to old age. Erikson characterizes these years as the years when it is normal for a human being to take an active concern for the next generation below his own. Frequently this concern involves one's own children, but it need not. There are many forms of caring for the next generation. The crisis is called a crisis of Generativity. Its counterquality is Stagnation.

2. Leadership and Followership (Leadership and Followership Vs. Authority Confusion)

If we think of youth as anticipating a future as a generative person, what form would this anticipation be likely to take? If you consider the middle or generative years to be years of responsibility and caring, then a youthful anticipation can readily be seen. It is as though youth can practice being responsible in anticipation of adulthood. Such practice can take the form of leadership in the world of youth, a leadership that shows a genuine concern for whoever is in tow behind the leader. Caring leadership, you might say. Since not all have the gift of being leaders, indeed, most people do not, Erikson describes a kind of independent and responsible approach to being led. I may not be at the head of the parade, but I can nevertheless make my own judgments about where and when I march. If I do, then I am an intelligent and ethical follower. I am preparing for a later stage in life when this independence will pay off in the role of parent, teacher, guide, or whatever form my contact with younger people may take.

3. Authority Confusion

What is the opposite of the caring leader or the independent follower? Put simply, the unscrupulous leader or the blind follower. The ability to lead provides its own peculiar platform of destruction. I can lead you down the primrose path to destruction. I can use my charm to use other people for my own gain without concern for the welfare of others. The dangers of being a blind and unthinking follower are obvious, for they are exactly the ones who invite manipulation and abuse on the part of their comrades. In both cases there is a misuse and misconception of authority. Blind followers regard people in leadership roles as having total authority and follow them without looking around. Unscrupulous leaders think their gifts of leadership entitle them to abuse other people; they use a position of authority to the hurt and destruction of others. I refer the reader again to the horizontal line of the chart in Appendix C for a schematic view of these crises in anticipation of the adult years.

4. The Struggle Within

And so, the struggle within once more, the seesaw between caring and abusing others. The microcosm within the person, the youthful Dr. Jekyll and Mr. Hyde, all within the same person. Out of the struggle, it is hoped, come the seeds of responsible caring for the young of the world when they themselves are older and in a position to be of use to those who are in the position where they themselves once were.

71

C. Anticipating Integrity/Despair

1. Integrity vs. Despair

And lastly, in anticipation of old age, Erikson's last stage, characterized by a crisis of Integrity. The word "integrity" connotes a sense of coherence or wholeness, as we have seen. The last stage in life is a battleground between gathering together the experiences of a lifetime into a coherent whole called wisdom, and the sense of despair attendant upon the realization that there won't be another chance to rectify yesterday's mistakes. How does youth look forward to the wisdom of old age?

2. Ideological Commitment

If old people struggle to stand up for their own values, the synthesis of a lifetime, it is the task of youth to begin the job of standing for something, looking back on the values learned in childhood, looking forward to adulthood's challenges, youth begins the vital task of finding out what she stands for and what she stands against. Erikson uses the phrase "Ideological Commitment vs. Confusion of Values" to describe the beginnings of value formation in youth.

We must begin with the word "ideological." It is the adjectival form of the noun, "ideology." What is an ideology? The dictionary meaning: "visionary theorising" and again, "the manner or content of thinking characteristic of an individual, group, or culture." What is Erikson's bias here? He says that every society offers an ideology or ideologies to its youth. He also speaks of an ideology as a worldview that is simpler than the world itself.

Putting it in other words, every country, every religion, every unit of people offers to its own young people a way of looking at right and wrong. Generally speaking, this way of looking at things is initially put to young people in a very boiled down form. A few examples: American culture offers its youth the vision of free enterprise in business, of democracy in politics, freedom in religion. Many American children are taught that hard work and persistence will bring success, sooner or later. Many American children are taught that financial success is basically success in life.

Those are a few ideologies offered youth in the U.S. today. There are lots of others. All ideologies, if Erikson is correct, are too simple. There are basically good ones and basically bad ones, yet all hold out promises of reward that are not quite what they say. All ideologies are a little slick; they mask the exceptions to the rule and pass over the possibility of failure in the vision of the promise. Generally, an ideology contains within itself the notion that those who follow it are "the elect," God's people, the chosen ones, or even a special, superior species of persons. For example: Some Americans regard themselves almost unconsciously as a sort of living measuring stick of all other peoples. The world being divided between Americans and "gooks" of one kind or another. The gooks are all of a lesser species.

With this rather chilling way of looking at ideology, Erikson unhesitatingly submits that Ideological Commitment of some form is essential to youth. He decidedly does not say that Ideological Commitment is necessary for older adults. His understanding is that youth needs something to be faithful to, to invest in, and that the rest of life is for finding out where the exceptions to the message are, its limitations and narrownesses. An old saying seems here apropos to his position: "If you don't stand for something, you'll fall for everything."

3. Adult Commitment: A Mature Ethic

Erikson expects a broader understanding of right and wrong from adults...and he is quite specific in pointing out that any mature ethic or religious belief must come to terms with the fact that its adherents are not the only "Chosen People." Put another way, you can be proud of your people, as long as you don't think their uniqueness makes them better than the rest of humankind. You can be convinced of your code and your cause, as long as you don't think your code is the only good one and that your cause is the only just one. A mature ethic demands acceptance of the existence of only one species, the human species, one overarching special people, the human people. A mature ethic admits of no super race, no super sex, and no super religion. The ideologies of youth nearly always are tainted with what might be called "the supers." It is the task of the adult years following youth to outgrow "the supers," and, incidentally, to remember that the young ones coming up have not yet outgrown them.

4. Value Confusion

The call for commitment to ideology is opposed by what Erikson calls "Value Confusion." Value Confusion is the state of not knowing what your values are. This confusion is a necessary part, however painful it may be in the beginning, to finding what you stand for. Like all the Eriksonian counterqualities, it is not reserved for "bad guys." It is a necessary part of the struggle, without which there can be no new values formed. Without this Confusion of Values, there is no chance for a later adult ethic, without it no chance for what might be called the final ethic, the wisdom of old age.

So, there it is, a look at the crisis of Identity as a renegotiation of all the crises of childhood and as an anticipation of all the crises of adulthood and old age.

D. Societal Factors of Identity

And is the crisis of Identity affected by societal factors? Obviously, the answer is "Yes." It takes no large jump of logic to see that if this crucial time in life recapitulates the crises before it in a special way and anticipates the crises to come, each of which has been deeply influenced by a person's societal milieu, then this stage of course will be a societal stage.

1. Gandhi

If we have seen the youthful Gandhi, living in an extended Indian family, marrying in an arranged marriage at the age of thirteen, affected throughout his boyhood with Hindu and Jain respect for life, if we have seen him as a student of English Law in London and distressed by the social injustices he witnessed in South Africa...and wondering what means could be used to raise the low place of his people, it should not come as a surprise that the Identity of Gandhi was a strange mixture of Indian and English, that as a reformer he was at once religious in an Eastern sense and political in a sense partly Eastern and partly Western.

2. Luther

Gandhi was a very Eastern reformer, just as Martin

74

Luther was a very German reformer. Luther was a reformer whose native German tongue...so silent in the Roman Church of his day, became the personification of Church reform. He brought a German church to Germany. His own regionalism became a model of religion. Luther translated the Bible into German; he translated religion into German. Who but the son of a father as patriarchal as his own could have thumbed his nose at the papacy of Rome with such anger as he showed.... The German family is famous for being dominated by the father. German sons through the ages have fought to be free from their own fathers and those who remind them of these fathers, only to become such same fathers themselves. If Gandhi brought India back to its own roots and away from English values, Luther brought Germany's Christians back to their own roots and language and away from the Latin of Rome as well as the peculiarly Roman Father, the Pope. Erikson's two great biographies are illuminations of just how much society affects the Identities of leaders it nourishes.

E. Later Forms of the Crisis of Identity

In another vein, one might ask, "Does the crisis of Identity have later forms? Can it reoccur later in life? Indeed it does. Erikson speaks of "the repeated adolescence of creative minds." Restless, and above all, creative people, seem to have to reassert their own Identities at regular intervals in later life.

1. Freud's Later Crisis of Identity

Sigmund Freud himself is an example. At the age of forty, Freud's Identity as a physician, an innovator, and the founder of a new kind of healing, was already firmly established. And yet he had a terrible dream of being a complete incompetent as a doctor. In the dream, he was held up to ridicule, because of his unusual methods of curing a patient. The patient herself remained ill after a seeming recovery. Freud was a fool. His reputation about to be lost, his very Identity at stake.

In the second half of the dream, he discovers that his accusers themselves are the incompetent ones. The trials of his patient are traced to the use of an infected needle by one of his interfering colleagues. Freud is exonerated. His hold on himself and his profession is restored.

What does the dream tell us? It is an indication to us that this daring physician's originality put him continually in the midst of controversy for most of his adult life. Far more than ordinary men, he was all his life the kind of person whose reputation was questioned repeatedly. His very originality led others to question him--and, of course, caused him to question himself.

The dream in question not only indicates how frequently he himself was shaken by the controversy around him. It also performed the valuable task of strengthening his own belief in himself. It reminded him forcibly of his own honesty and skill. It serves to remind us that creative people frequently have to renew their youthful struggles for Identity in later years, if for no other reason than the fact that they are so often questioned by less perceptive people.

2. William James' Identity Crisis at Sixty

Another Identity dream cited by Erikson was a dream that the famous American psychologist and philosopher William James had when he was in his sixties, not long before his death.

James as a young man had spent a very long time finding himself and his niche in life as a researcher. He had tried many occupations and had nearly gone crazy attempting to find some occupation that fit. He was thirty years of age before he finally found himself and his life's work.

Now, late in life, a famous author, a distinguished psychologist, a respected philosopher, he has a dream reawakening his years of frustration and upset, when as a young man he had no idea where he was going. That had been a time in his life which seemed filled with nothing but failure and depression. All this came back to him as an old man in the dream.

He relates that he awoke to find himself, despite the evidence of a distinguished life, once again feeling lost and at sea, leading a meaningless life, a life essentially wasted and profitless.

There was one difference between this dream and the time of his youth...and that difference was vital. He could remember that as a young man he had actually found himself, no matter what his feelings on waking up from this terrible dream. He knew that he had overcome

76

this confusion once before--and that if he had done it
once, he might well do it again.

He relates that this nightmare's mood did indeed
pass, but that it remained for him a powerful reminder
in his old age not only of the struggles of his own
youth, but of the struggles of the young people with
whom he himself was working as an old man. This
harrowing dream rekindled in James an empathy for
young students and enabled him to show a "grand"
fatherly care, born of his own reexperience as an old
man of the trials of being young.

In conclusion, we may note that a serious student
of Erik Erikson will find it no surprise that any stage
in life should surface in a new form later, for in the
Eriksonian scheme of things we are, each of us, the
product, among other things, of our own life histories.

F. Earlier Forms of the Crisis of Identity

Do earlier stages somehow look forward to the
Crisis of Identity? Indeed...and one stage in
particular stands out here, the third, or oedipal
stage, Initiative vs. Guilt. One can call it the
first stage in which a person makes something of
herself, and this is in the face of the guilt attendant
upon fathers or mothers who want to keep the small
person in her place. It is the first stage of finding
a parent as a rival in what I want to do, sometimes a
punitive rival, always a powerful rival. This is the
beginning of an assessment of what I have going for me,
and what I am going to do with it. These two questions
become the hallmark of the later youthful quest of
identity, previewed, as it were, by the toddler.

There are echoes of the crisis of Identity, then,
extending all through a person's life, some
anticipatory, others retrospective. In this second
part of our treatment of Identity, we have completed a
sort of bird's eye view of the whole life cycle, each
stage of which we have treated separately in another
place. We have completed our treatment of the eight
stages. By way of denouement, a word, looking back,
on a term used throughout the treatment of all the
stages, the word "crisis."

G. Once Again, the Crisis

If each of the eight stages is characterized by a

certain inner competition, Trust vs. Mistrust, Intimacy vs. Isolation, the word "crisis" adds specificity to the struggle, so much at the heart of every Eriksonian stage. We wish to underline this key concept once more at the end of this section of the book.

In a competition, one always asks, "Who is going to win?" In a mismatch, one party dominates the other, while in a really worthy game, there is a real tussle between two or more opposing players or teams. In this context, the word "crisis." Erikson notes that "crisis" no longer denotes impending disaster or catastrophe. He sees the term as today designating "a necessary turning point, a crucial moment, when development must move one way or another, marshalling resources of growth, recovery, and further differentiation."

Each stage then is a special turning point in human development. The inner competition of each stages does not carry with it any assurance that either of the opposing qualities will triumph. It underlines that there will be a struggle between two, no matter what the outcome. It carries the hope that the positive quality will eventually get the upper hand, but it underlines the idea that there can be no triumph without an opponent. In a crisis as Erikson uses the word, there can be no triumph without a struggle.

There are no shutouts in the inner contests of Erik Erikson. The life cycle at every point is marked by tension and competition within the person. His vision of human living is one of continual struggle from birth to death. His hope is that the struggle will be zestful and creative and that productive, caring people will stem from this struggle. There is nothing static in his view of human life. His descriptions of it have a dynamic quality of never being finished. There is no attempt on his part to say the last word. His books are always "to be continued." They can be called sketches of life, always holding out the possibility of a new and better picture. And so, in the spirit of Erik Erikson, we will end this description of the life cycle, not with a period but with a semicolon, as evidence that the work will never be over.

We have ended but not completed a general overview of his work here. A series of more particular chapters is to follow, putting the theory to work. We will

READINGS SUGGESTED BY THIS CHAPTER

Besides the readings suggested at the end of the earlier chapter on Identity, I would refer the reader to Chapter Ten of Childhood and Society, "The Legend of Maxim Gorky's Youth." The reference to Sigmund Freud's later crisis of Identity, as well as that of William James', is from Identity: Youth and Crisis, Chapter IV, 5.

CHAPTER VII

PLAY, TOYS, AND WORK

A. The Play of Children

The whole idea of play is an important one for Erik Erikson. His early work as a child psychoanalyst centered on close observation of troubled children at play. Very often, the play of children spoke to him a language of great clarity of the source of their upset as well as avenues for cure. Erikson points out that childhood play is quite different from the play of adults, as we have seen in Chapter Two. The sports and games of grownups provide a way of stepping aside into another world apart from the world of work. Children use play, not so much to step aside from normal life as to step forward to new mastery. Children use play to anticipate real life situations. They imagine themselves being firefighters and wrestlers, football players, super heroes, librarians. Anything that is a possible future role they can try on. Play is a form of practicing for future events. I might add that it also is a way of evening the scores for battles lost. Kids lose a lot of battles with mothers and fathers, brothers and sisters and friends. In imagination and drama they can set things right again. You can win battles lost in your play and thereby get your cool back.

The age of play, par excellence for Erikson, is his age of the preschooler, roughly of the ages of three to five, entitled Initiative vs. Guilt. Work has not yet come as a regular part of life. The day is spent in play. This is the age of running and jumping and exploring. It is the age in which one dreams of competing against one's same sex parent for the affections of the other one. Play enables you to do things you could never get away with outside the world of imagination and acting out.

The great gift of playing things out is that its very make-believe quality brings with it a kind of freedom from guilt and fear. The song says, "It doesn't cost you anything to dream." Active four and five year olds explore all sorts of forbidden territories in their play and in the process build up an ability and a confidence for "real" events. Children play out what they hope to be later; they learn tactics and confidence. Perhaps most important, they preserve and develop a sense of boldness and initiative in a make-believe world by trying out roles in make-believe; where no one will retaliate or make them feel guilty. Children practice at life in their games the same way that older people practice their ground strokes for tennis or rehearse beforehand proposals for marriage.

It is basic to this understanding of the importance of childhood's play for parents to understand that premature introductions into the world of work deprive children of vital practice time for other things. Early entrance into schooling in order for a child "to get ahead" might have just the opposite effect. For it is by play that a child puts her world together. Play time is not wasted time: it is vital time. Its loss will be a vital loss. Children who are deprived of time for play are often children who lose a vital sense of initiative. Play and trying new things go together. A too-early introduction into the world of work can make Jack a very dull boy indeed, for in later years his life may be robbed of a playful zest and creativeness so important in a fully alive human being, keeping his nose to the grindstone with such grimness in the name of morality that the opportunities he might have noticed will pass him by. Playfulness in later life is anchored in childhood's make-believe... and playfulness, the willingness to experiment, is vital not only in childhood's make-believe but in youth's long dreams.

B. The Play of Youth

Another key stage in the life cycle where playful initiative is vital for human development is the stage of Identity vs. Identity Confusion...the time between childhood and being an adult. If youth is a time in life characterized by a search for something worth being faithful to, it follows that the search should be given time. The whole notion of "moratorium" is germane here. A moratorium is a period of delay in which youth can give itself the freedom to take a long look at childhood's identifications and adulthood's promises. A sort of second preschool age given to playful experiments in different roles and fields. In the world of love, a time for playing the field. It takes time to find out what you stand for and you generally don't find out what that is with your first cause, your first love, or, for that matter, your first job or college major.

This author has written elsewhere of his fear of premature closure of this period of delay. There is a kind of death-dealing sincerity in the teenager who "has always known what she wanted to be." Childhood sweethearts are seldom the right ones. A society with a work ethic in its history needs to be reminded that playful experimentation on the part of youth is a very vital preparation for a vigorous and interested life of work in years to come. Work without enthusiasm is drudgery. A certain playfulness is necessary in choosing a fitting life of work and it is important even after the choice has been made, as we shall see.

C. Mature Playfulness

One might think that by adulthood, young or old, that the playfulness of the child as well as the frolicsome experimentations of youth in search of Identity should be put firmly behind the adult in his or her responsible attempts to care for the next generation, so aptly called by Erikson, Generativity. An indication that he might see things otherwise is contained in the introduction to a book on play and its significance for human living, entitled by Erikson, Toys and Reasons.

In that introduction to his most complete treatment of the matter of play and playfulness, Erikson quotes Plato as saying that play is linked in Greek with the word "to leap." Although adult leaping and capering about is generally more likely to be in tune with a game of tennis than it is to be associated with the workplace, nevertheless, the joy of leaping about is associated by Erikson with the world of the adult. There is a certain quality in the work of creative people that is allied to the play of the child. Child's play of its essence is an improvisation, an act of imagination. Creative people never leave this quality behind. Erikson cites the work of Albert Einstein as an example. Einstein was a very creative and imaginative physicist who wove his theories in the world of theoretical physics with all the artistry of a child, not letting adult concerns as to just how each theoretical concept might or might not be useful to the world bother his theorizing. Gandhi was a very playful politician; the man who had been a tease as a little boy, teased the British forces of occupation unmercifully with no more weapons than a teasing child has. There is a certain childlike simplicity in an adult who dares any scenario and is free to dream any dream. In one of his last major works, Erikson has written a monologue on the Gospels. He finds the Gospel injunction "Unless you become as little children, you shall not enter the Kingdom of Heaven" as speaking to this quality of playfulness, of simplicity, of wide-ranging imagination that he sees as so necessary a quality in human adults.

Just as play gives hope to a child, just as childhood's world of tiny dramatizations gives vision to what the child may one day be, so the playfulness and imagination of the adult allows persons in the grownup world to see visions and dream dreams. Today's world, says Erikson, needs all the vision it can get. Such vision is normally not the fruit of mere conscientiousness. It is vision that allows one to see the broad scene, what lies beneath the surface, how past history may be reapplied to modern times. A playfulness that is rooted in childhood and rediscovered in the search for Identity is the source of adult vision.

D. Play and Old Age

If the task of most of adulthood is caring for the next generation, in some way being fatherly or motherly, what for those at the end of adulthood, grown men and women who have retired, whose children have grown up themselves, those who in some sense are "grand" fathers and mothers. Does the play of childhood have any purchase on them?

Indeed, yes. There is a quite ultimate form of playfulness that seeks to provide vision through improvisation for the end of life and what may come after that. Just as children's daily, small, dramatic games rehearse for future roles and keep past failures in perspective, so it is with the old ones, whose life crisis is termed by Erikson, Integrity vs. Despair. If children seek to integrate the beginnings of their lives by play, so it is for old people, with a whole lifetime to integrate. Old people have as well a future equally as opaque as adulthood is to a child.

Some sort of imaginative unification of one's past life is what stands between an old person and despair. It takes vision to look back as well as to look forward. If play gives vision and hope to a small child, Erikson sees a playful attitude and the vision it engenders as giving faith to an old person. Old age provides a sort of detachment well suited to putting

86

aside earlier adulthood's heavy cares. With this
opportunity for lightening adulthood's burden can come,
when one might least expect it, a chance to leap and
jump in one's imagination, a chance for a vision unen-
cumbered with "watching the store" and yet carrying
with it a lifetime of experience. There is a chance to
look with new eyes not only at the pages of the diary
of a lifetime but to look again at what may come after
death.

E. Play and Ritualism

1. Style and Society

As we have looked at play and playfulness as a
quality of life necessary at every stage, there has
been a notable omission. We have not spoken of
society. Every child, every adolescent, and every
adult lives in a society of some kind. The reader
will not be surprised that Erik Erikson's treatment of
play and playfulness does not leave the societal
dimension out. That dimension is basic to this work.

The drama, the make-believe so important to small
children, takes place in families, in communities,
among peoples and nations.

Families have a way of giving a style to the small
interactions that occur day in and day out. Groups of
all kinds produce small formalities which can provide a
sort of husk for the seeds of creativity and playfulness. There is a preservative character in these small
styles which Erik Erikson calls "ritualizations." As
though creativity and playfulness are always in danger
of being engulfed in the tares of this world. A family
style provides a toughness and durability to play.
Families have special ways of greeting each other,
special expressions, small ways of recognition.
Different peoples have different ways, peculiar to
them, for the play of children. The small styles of
schooling children vary, but any system that is a good
one will reward good performance in a way that is
consonant with one's people and a child's creativity.

The styles given by different peoples to a
moratorium between childhood and adulthood vary
greatly. Still, every society, if Erikson is correct,
provides a time of delay for its youth in which to
construct something unique from the remnants of her
childhood and the expectations of her people for

87

adulthood. The different affiliative styles of lovers, the different structures of family union, the acceptable styles of old age--all, in a healthy community, serve to provide a certain continuity to one's life within which to exercise a degree of playful inventiveness. A society or family so rigid as to allow no leeway in its small customs is stifling. A society or family without customary ways is chaotic. Societies provide structure. Although structures can be stifling in the small ways of living, any form of consistent family or community life vanishes without them. They are the stuff of creativity.

2. Americans: Ritualism and Continuity

A society of immigrants as American society inevitably is, has given rise to a vision of the human person, once termed "the self-made man." We Americans like to think of ourselves as a classless society. "Anybody can be President in the United States," we say.

Whether that is true or not is not the point; if we think of ourselves as self-made people we could well forget the importance of a continuity of ritualisms and become a rootless people or a chameleonlike people, as devoid of creativity as of ethics. This chapter has the connection between work and play as its subject. A continuity of family and societal ritualisms are vital for a creative way of working. Who you are is never separate from your family and your country. How you work depends a great deal on knowing who you are. Whether you are honest and caring does too, but these latter two are ethical concerns to be picked up in a chapter at the end of this book.

Much of Erikson's theory ends in a consideration of right and wrong, almost as if all the strands of his system end in a consideration of how people get along with each other and with the fruit of their labor. Right and wrong, good and evil are such a concern in Erikson's vision of the life cycle of humankind that this author prefers to have introduced each strand before discussing the connection between developing people and a sense of right and wrong.

If this chapter has concerned itself with the importance of play and playfulness in human development with specific emphasis on the world of

88

work, there are other important connections between play and the specificities of life. There is a vital connection between play and whether one is man or woman, male or female.

READINGS SUGGESTED BY CHAPTER SEVEN

The reader of <u>Childhood and Society</u> will at this point, I hope, want to reread Chapter Six of that book, entitled, "Toys and Reasons."

The material for this chapter is taken in large part from Erikson's book on play and playfulness, <u>Toys and Reasons</u>. The references to Gandhi's playfulness are from <u>Gandhi's Truth</u>. The reference to my own work on playfulness and youth is from <u>Passages In Teaching</u>, Chapters One and Three. Erikson's comments on playfulness in the Gospels are made in <u>The Yale Review</u>, Volume 70, No. 3, April, 1981.

As for references to playfulness in the literature of children, I would again refer the reader to the books of Maurice Sendak, as well as Mordecai Richler's story of a small boy's imagination, <u>Jacob Two Two Meets the Hooded Fang</u>.

A discerning reader might take a second look at the playfulness and high jinks in <u>Romeo and Juliet</u> and even in the melancholy Dane himself. Other examples of playfulness during the crisis of Identity are clearly in evidence in all the films mentioned in the readings for the first chapter on adolescence.

As for playfulness among mature adults, one may note in passing that in many of Shakespeare's plays, it is the jester or fool who tells the truth which escapes most of the play's characters. Confer the fool in <u>King Lear</u> and Sir Toby Belch in <u>Twelfth Night</u>.

Playful people who see the truth in our own time run from Bill Cosby to Irma Bombeck, from Gandhi to Einstein. I refer the reader to Cosby's monologues, to Bombeck's books and newspaper columns, but not to $E=MC^2$, the playful contribution of Albert Einstein to world physics.

CHAPTER VIII

MALE AND FEMALE

A. Studies at Berkley

What does Erik Erikson have to say about the differences between men and women? There's no doubt in his mind that there are differences. Each person, without exception, is marked by having a body, a history, and the ability to make a working whole from these two.

Erikson's two-year study at the Institute of Child Welfare at Berkley, California, is evidence of this biological and cultural interpretation of male and female. He observed carefully the play of a large group, nearly five hundred boys and girls. They ranged in age between eleven and thirteen. They were normal, healthy, middle-class children in the years just preceding adolescence. The kids, one at a time, were given a set of ordinary blocks, the kind children use for play the world over. They were provided as well with small dolls representing men and women of varying ages and occupation. Lastly, they were given toy cars and trucks. With these "tools", they were instructed to make an exciting scene, like a set in a movie.

Each child made three scenes: Erikson himself watched, took notes, drew sketches of the work, as each project progressed. Patterns began to emerge as more and more children's scenes were put together. The boys generally made outdoor scenes with lots of motion, featuring street scenes, traffic, collisions. The structures they made tended to be high with protruding ornaments; there was often a danger of collapse.

The girls were more likely to make house interiors or enclosures with low walls. These interiors were generally peaceful; sometimes animals or men would intrude into the peaceful interior.

What conclusions did Erikson draw? That the play constructions were each unique, reflecting each child's individuality. The constructions were clearly cultural as well, reflecting what each child was expected by his family or her family to be now, as well as in times to come. Along with uniqueness and the expectations of culture was evidence that the basic male or female groundplan of body was reflected as well.

91

The male children's concern with movement, collisions, and intrusions was in contrast to the females' concern with interiors, with peace. More than thirty years after this work, Erikson wrote, in response to critics Elizabeth Janeway and Kate Millet, that he was well aware that both males and females have bodily interiors and live in houses. An interpretation of his long since completed study on the play of preadolescent girls and boys was not meant to indicate that women alone concerned themselves with peace, intuition, and the interior life. He pointed out as well that both boys and girls walk and stand upright, and are given to sticking their noses into areas of life other than home and hearth.

It is much too simple to interpret this study as saying that females are all inner people because their biological equipment is more concave than men's. Women have vaginas and men have penises, it is true. But cultural expectations have a lot to do with what children play at, not to mention the numerous small boys who built scenes more like the typical girl's scenes and the girls who built scenes of lively action in the street.

Erikson concerned himself with the rich interplay between bodily carriage or form and the content of the scenes. He bluntly underlines that everybody has a body, that that body has a lot to do with being "somebody" in particular. Sex differences are important, rock-bottom bodily differences, besides being individual and cultural.

B. Feminist Suspicion and American Attitudes

Erikson feels that much of the early feminist suspicion of his underlining sexual differences as important in understanding persons is because he, after all, is a male commentator, and males are certainly part of the problem of the emancipation of women. He feels, as well, that it is an American characteristic, male and female, to regard all options in human life as open to everybody. Any restriction of opportunity is seen as at least unAmerican and probably evil. We are a people who left a continent behind to start afresh and we regard that freshness as sacred. However, common sense should tell us that even in the Land of the Free, there is a division of talent. Male or female, my body is a part of this talent. So is my family, the times I live in, and where I come from.

As a part of the individuation that makes each person unique and special is one's sexuality.

It is Erik Erikson's persuasion that sexuality is a prime factor in providing hope for the world we live in. Far from seeing women's characteristics as limiting, he sees a bent of mind and body concerned with interiority and peace as desperately needed in a world still dominated by the grownup versions of the ten year old boy, intent upon warfare, competition, and the indiscriminate use of the world's dwindling resources. Erikson is emphatic in stating that unless the grownup versions of the ten year old girls--who concerned themselves with approachability, harmony, and peace--can bring these values into the public arena of business and politics, the good old boys of this world may well leave little peace or resources for their sons and daughters in times to come.

C. Man's Limitations and Women

Women, in short, are unique, and in a certain sense limited, just as men are. Erikson is far more concerned with what he sees to be the limitations of man's imagination in today's technological society than he is with the so-called "limitations" of women.

As for the negative self-images so many women feel is part of contemporary American society's gift to them, Erikson has this to say. It seems inevitable that American females often learn as they grow up that the world values very fully all those activities associated with having a man's so-called magic wand--action, adventure, change, fighting, building and throwing your weight around generally. Intuition, peace-making and compassion are not rewarded as much as those outer values. Being a person more inner than outer is not highly valued in a "can do" society or even a consumer society. A person, man or woman, who is basically compassionate is often not a good competitor or a showy consumer.

D. Emotional Ecology: Deals

If we are concerned with the inner economy of male and female and how it is accepted by society, it is only a short jump from here to what Erikson calls "emotional ecology." Where one sex harbors negative images of the other, usually both are the losers. Accomodations are made in family life, for example.

Many a father has given a vital part of what he has to give to his children to his wife, thus impoverishing himself. In return, he gets to be the lion outside the home, giving a disproportionate amount of time "making it" away from home while losing much of his own gift as a parent. His wife, then, is the tabby cat at work but very much a lioness at home. Erikson points out that "deals" such as this one are seldom recognized for what they are by the parties themselves. He regards understanding and insight as vital in the liberation of both women and men.

Consider the predicament of a boy who is intuitive or compassionate or kind; most boys must learn to suppress in themselves those characteristics considered "not manly" or worse yet, "effeminate." The conflict within a boy who has received his ideal from his mother, only to discover that what is so close to the core of his being is not suitable for a man.

Consider a small girl who feels inferior because of her boy companions' hatred and confusion over their own tender hearts. What they find unacceptable in themselves, of course, they vilify in others. Erikson sees both men and women as agonized over not being able to "borrow" each other's stereotyped sexual characteristics, and yet--and this is key--this confinement is most often unrecognized.

E. Historical Perspectives

A word on history. Frequently in these pages, I have attempted to spell out <u>which</u> men and <u>which</u> women in <u>which</u> times. This is an attempt on my part to keep on the printed page the ever-present concern of Erik Erikson with the times we live in, and those in the context of the times before. History, a personal approach to history, postulates that every personal problem has a history. The struggle of American women today has a history and, if Erikson is right, makes sense only in terms of that history. History lets you know in a special way where your strengths are and where you have been shortchanged. Knowing her own history gives an individual person a chance for a certain consistency in growing up, a chance to say, "These are my people" and "I am a part of their struggle." It is the concern for history on the part of a psychoanalyst that is striking here. A reader would perhaps expect a concern for personal history or case history, but Erikson's concern, here in a treatment of men and women, is that contemporary men and women realize how deeply we are affected by the American Revolution, the Declaration of Independence, the Frontier, the moving of rural men and women into the city, the advent of technology in the home and workplace. The American psyche in a psychohistorical framework is the subject of our next chapter, but it remains important here to underline that a certain very American contempt for history is lethal when it comes to bringing insight to bear upon the situation of the sexes in contemporary America. The people who burned witches in New England are the ancestors of those who kept Mom in the kitchen in the forties. The restless men of the American frontier are the ancestors of the commuter Dads of the nineteen fifties and sixties. Neither were "at home" when they were home. The black women who bore and raised black children in the South of slave days, without the help of husbands, are the ancestors of a matriarchal black society that is becoming more and more the object of concern in the nineteen eighties. We do have a past and it can help uncover the deceptions of the present if we study it. It can provide, as well, a sense of continuity of strengths, the deeper because we have seen them in our own people who lived before us.

F. Exhaustion and Reform

It is a rootless and uninformed sense of outrage over the injustices between men and women in today's society that Erikson fears as likely to die of exhaustion or to degenerate into a kind of moralistic name-calling. Dividing the world into good guys and bad guys is an old trick for getting people ready to fight, but in the long run a cold look at the deals and collusions of both sexes as they exist in history has a better chance for real liberation of both sexes than the vindication of one.

G. Masochism: Male and Female

Of the more celebrated "deals" between the sexes in early psychoanalytic literature is the issue of female masochism. What does Erikson do with it? His approach is configurational; he won't let you leave out the whole picture. Neither male nor female, for example, has a corner on selfinflicted suffering. True, Erikson believes that a bodily carriage which accentuates inner space contains potentially a kind of inner strength that is capable of enduring pain and

95

suffering out of inner strength. Most males have only the vaguest notion of the pain involved in bearing a child, to name one obvious example of inner strength born of inner life. Still, only when other forces have infantilized women, or prostituted them or immobilized them, has a perverted form of the ability to withstand pain become prominent among women.

Man's masochism is not discussed in classical psychoanalytic literature, but Erikson will not let his students escape without considering the savage way men have done themselves in by the exploitation of the masculine propensity for exploring outer spaces. Hidden under the deceptive imagery of heroism, duty, and work, men have slaughtered each other in warfare, surrendered their roles as fathers of families, and dulled their consciences as regards the ethic of the working place. Men themselves are the losers. And, of course, the further tragedy is that the absentee father, the ruthless competitor, and the soldier obsessed with war rarely recognize the self-destroying properties of their obsessions.

H.   Contemporary Technology and the Sexes

No historical approach to the relations between the sexes, even a brief overview such as this one, should be without reference to the impact of technology on the lives of men and women. I will give two examples of the effect of technology which will here have to serve as symbols of a more complicated scenario.

1.   Birth Control

For women, technology has meant the advent of accessible and effective birth control. If motherhood was once used to enslave women by the combined forces of instinctual drive, social tradition, and inner collusion, the power of being able to plan parenthood has suddenly cut through much of the physical onus of the large family. A liberation, an ecological necessity and a challenge. The challenge, as Erikson sees it, is the challenge to be a generative person in a world which makes possible the limitation or elimination of biological motherhood. Erikson is here concerned with the possible overlooking, on the part of contemporary women and men, of the deep-seated human need to turn one's middle years to the support of the younger generation.

He is concerned about the shallow lives of people whose middle years center upon themselves, "liberated" by the magic of birth control. Middle-class playboys and playmates have lives just as empty as their more celebrated jet set counterparts. Birth control will be a liberation only if those who use it concern themselves in an active way for the children of other families and other nations as a prime focus for their middle years.

As with birth, which I have listed as "woman's problem" because women <u>do bear</u> the children, so with arms, a "man's problem" because men generally are the ones who bear the arms. That both sexes are involved in problems of birth control and arms control is, I hope, clear.

2. War

Technology has changed, probably forever, the role of arms and warfare in the lives of men, and women. Wars have always been incomplete by nature, leaving the door open for other wars, where men can, in the next generation, affirm their masculinity, impress their comrades, their enemy, and their women. If Erikson is right, men will have to borrow some of the inner concerns more typical of women—concerns for harmony and peace, not just within the family but in the families of nations—if humankind is to survive the weapons technology has given us. A recognition on the part of men that what women (and particularly mothers) have stood for throughout the ages—a hatred of the killing involved in war—must become man's heritage as well. A cold assessment of the impersonal efficiency of modern weaponry is needed. Erikson feels that without women standing in public for what they have always stood for in private—providing an alternative to the male imagination—there will be no peace. Nor does he leave out the hope that in a future world, where men and women may be more free to acknowledge the parts of themselves traditionally the exclusive prerogative of the other sex, both women and men will be the winners. Birth control carries with it an obligation to continue to be caring; arms control carries the hope that caring can extend to people who were once thought of as the enemy.

Our society, our world, demands that men acknowledge the feminine aspects of themselves, that women in the public arena not forget that they are women even in areas once traditionally masculine. These ethical issues are basic to survival and can only be resolved with the help of understanding and insight.

I. Conclusions

In conclusion to this overview of Erikson's thoughts on the sexes, we need to repeat what is clear. In girls, a certain "inner-directedness" and a certain self-contained strength and peace has been cultivated in our society. They have often been forced to abandon, and sometimes later to overdo, much early locomotor vigor, social and intellectual initiative and intrusiveness, which (potentially) girls share with boys.

With boys, in pursuing the male role beyond what comes naturally, our society has inculcated a necessity for them to dissimulate and disavow what receptivity and intuitiveness they (potentially) share with girls. Each sex has overdeveloped what it has been given by nature, and has had to compensate for what it has had to deny. Each sex in our society has gotten credit for this divided self-image. To what extent oppressor and oppressed collude with each other in both flattering and enslaving each other and themselves--these are the issues contemporary women and men need to confront, to discuss, to uncover. In the process, the basic insights of psychoanalysis about the unconscious mind should not be neglected...because unknowing self-deception is at the heart of the problem.

RECOMMENDED READINGS FOR THIS CHAPTER

Erik Erikson writes a lot about men and women. The reader of Childhood and Society will find rich material concerning the sexes in Chapter Two of that book, entitled, "The Theory of Infantile Sexuality." This section of the book contains the seeds of most of his later writings on the differences between male and female. Included is a report on his celebrated study of ten to twelve year old boys and girls done at the Institute of Child Welfare in Berkley, California during the nearly nineteen forties.

Chapter Eight, "Reflections on the American Identity," contains his characterization of American mothers and fathers of the nineteen forties.

As for the sources of the chapter you have just read, the main content for this chapter has come from two separate chapters in two separate books: Identity: Youth and Crisis, "Womanhood and Inner Space," and Life History and the Historical Moment, Part Three, II, "Once More the Inner Space."

Both of these chapters are controversial, the second one being a restatement of the first with roughly ten years in between writings. The second piece was written in nineteen seventy-five, in response to critics within the women's movement, specifically Betty Friedan and Elizabeth Janeway.

The response of feminist writers to Erikson's work reminds me once more of a recent book that I have already recommended to the reader concerned with the Identity, development and ethics of women. Its title: In a Different Voice by Carol Gilligan.

Gilligan is very critical of a whole sweep of writers on human development. The list includes Freud, Piaget, Kohlberg, Levinson, and Vaillant, as well as Erik Erikson. The main criticism levelled against each of these theorists is that each had a pronouncedly male bias in his descriptions of human development. Erikson's pioneering work on Identity, Intimacy, and Generativity is given its due as being more consonant with male and female development than any of the others. In many ways, this book is a tribute to the stature of Erik Erikson, as well as a complaint that he does not map female development with the clarity and completeness that he does for males.

99

It's a good book!

Excursions into the literary world of male and female are treacherous. There is a great variety of men, a large diversity of women. So—only an indication for the reader: Don Quixote pointing his magic spear at the windmill...the women of St. Luke's Gospel, so central to hearing the message of peace.

A very hesitant recommendation in modern writers—the women in Margaret Laurence's novels and stories have touched this author, as have the men in the novels of Graham Greene and Bernard Malamud.

CHAPTER IX

THE AMERICAN IDENTITY

A. Placing Our Remarks

A discussion of male and female in Erikson's work rather inevitably leads to a discussion of Americans in general, for most of his life's work has been spent studying the people of his adopted land. Granted, he has studied a bewildering variety of Americans-- Indians, submariners, blacks, students, immigrants, distressed people in all social classes of this country. He has studied and worked with American children, adolescents, middle-aged and old people. It has been observed elsewhere in this book that much of his work has been concerned with normal development. His very first book contains a chapter entitled, "Reflections on the American Identity." There have been reflections on the American character in one form or another in most of his books.

This particular overview of his work will concentrate on his later comments on the American people, both because they are closer to the times in which this book is written and because of the striking way in which Erikson has used early American history in his analysis. Any summary of his work should insist on historical bias as being central to his work. His writings of the nineteen seventies underline history so boldly and clearly that they illustrate well this historical concern.

1. "Identity" in this Context

A word on the meaning of the word Identity as he here uses it. He uses the term broadly. In other contexts he has used it narrowly, to indicate a particular stage in the life cycle, Stage Five, called Identity versus Identity Confusion. In that context, he refers specifically to a particular time in life, the time between childhood and adulthood. The time of youth or adolescence. Here, a broader use of the term.

Here, the term refers to a perduring character. Erikson himself says:

> A sense of identity means a sense
> of being at one with oneself as one
> grows and develops; and it means,

101

> at the same time a sense of affinity
> with a <u>community's</u> sense of being at
> one with <u>its</u> future as well as its
> history.*

The context is overtly historical. He makes a connection between the Americans of the nineteen seventies with the Americans of the seventeen seventies, the Founding Fathers and the revolutionary American community around them two hundred years ago.

2. Erikson as Critic

Although in this context Erikson's remarks are made mainly in criticism, the reader of this book should remember that Erikson is himself an immigrant, that America is his own chosen country, and that his comments are made as one within the family who cares about it. In his own words, then:

> How the American way of life, with
> its singular industriousness and
> amiability, its teamwork, precision,
> and routinization, its special brand
> of courage and its inventive
> competitiveness, its playfulness and
> showmanship struck me as an immigrant
> and as therapist and student of
> children, I have recorded here and
> there, in my earlier writings.

Writing then, in the midst of the national turmoil of Watergate and the Viet Nam war, times of student riots and black unrest and a resurgence of feminism, he was writing at a time when the soul of America was peculiarly visible and vulnerable. It was as though the whole country was the embodiment of a patient seeking the healing insight of a gifted therapist. And indeed, it seems to this writer that Erikson was very much a therapist, very much a psychoanalyst in his remarks written during this period.

B. Thomas Jefferson and the Founding Fathers

1. New Man

Erikson begins one of his treatises on the American Identity with a discussion of Thomas

* Emphasis mine

102

Jefferson and the other founding fathers of the Revolutionary War period in American history.

Thomas Jefferson and the other founders of the Republic regarded themselves as "new men", as self-made men, denying implicitly and very explicitly in the American Revolution, the English Fatherland. They had made an Exoduslike crossing of the seas to a new Promised Land. They taught their followers to abandon old English loyalties. Erikson himself, in another context, reflects on the trauma of leaving Europe a century and a half later. The bitter taste of uprootedness is known to every immigrant, himself included. He speaks eloquently of the perduring guilt of the immigrant over the decision to leave the old country. The first Americans knew both the trauma of departure and the guilt of the decision to separate themselves from England.

2. A Chosen People

They made themselves a sort of new "Chosen People," different from those of the "old country." It has been an American characteristic ever since that time to regard the American people as "God's elect"...a sort of New Israel. And so the notion of a new and superior species arose, a kind of make-believe superiority to all outsiders. Indeed, this "pseudospecies" was restricted not only to Americans, but to American men, white men--in fact, white, Protestant men. The founding fathers were more concerned with the equality of men than women, whites more than blacks, and, to be sure, whites more than Indians.

This self-made quality contained within itself the need to keep some people down. The trauma of leaving, the guilt of repudiating England and Europe, carried with it a price. That price was a proclivity to assuage this guilt by keeping some available, close at hand people in their place, and they did so with a vengeance...neatly projecting their own arrogance and guilt upon those least able to defend themselves, and most close at hand.

3. Restoring the Earthly Paradise

If the Founding Fathers all bought one form or other of the Puritan theme of restoring the Earthly Paradise, if as God's elect, they felt called upon to make a new Garden of Eden, it is easy to understand how they embraced a way of looking at things that demanded hard work. Hard work, after all, was a sign of being members of God's Predestined. Hard work has been the price of identification with the American people ever since. This work ethic brought with it an emphasis on the future rather than the past. It helped the process of repudiating old codes of life and old loyalties from home countries left behind. The new men (and the new women, but with less credit) were hard workers, suspicious of intellectuals, especially those intellectuals who were concerned with history and roots. They tried their best to forget the past and didn't want to be reminded of it. Americans and the American Dream centered on the future.

C. The Inheritors of Jefferson's Dream

And how did the dreams of these Founding Fathers work out for those Americans living in this Promised Land two hundred years later? How about the inheritors of the Dream?

1. Suspicious of Play

By and large, America has retained its suspicion of play over work. We push our children to earlier and earlier school, so that the important part--the work part of life--can start earlier. We are prone to forget the importance of play for children, because we have still alive and well in our midst, the work ethic of our founders.

Because we are suspicious of history, most of us are still unaware of the connection between the work ethic of the past and the premium on work and jobs in the present. As a people, we are still very suspicious of a time of delay between childhood and adulthood, a time of playful experimentation with future roles. Erikson calls this time in life the "Crisis of Identity" and he sees the disaster of beginning an adulthood too quickly in the name of getting the job done. Without this period of experiment, the job is likely to be the wrong job, unsuited to one's talent.

2. Moralizers

Erikson feels that the need of the first Americans to keep somebody down is still very much with us. In the seventies, he observed very astutely

that the loudest moralizers are people who invariably
have made deals with their own consciences. In retro-
spect, one is struck by how many of the politicians who
ran on the law-and-order ticket of the Nixon presiden-
tial campaigns of sixty-eight and seventy-two were
later found to have committed flagrant violations of
the law in those very campaigns featuring a law-and-
order plank. Not by chance, says Erik Erikson. We
have a long history of removing our own guilt by
punishing other people.

3. Contentious People

If the colonists blamed their troubles on England
long ago, they laid the framework for a long history
of blamers in their wake. We are a contentious people
and we came by this quality honestly; it began with
the American Revolution. Contrition is not an
American virtue.

4. Workers

And the Earthly Paradise? Do modern Americans
still work for it? It is not so much the work itself;
we are still a working people. It is somehow the
notion that nothing else counts except work. If the
early Americans were suspicious of the lands of their
origins, later Americans tend to think that they have
nothing to learn from their families, ethnic groups,
and common cultures. There is a danger of a loss of
continuity, a loss of pride, a certain rootlessness
and absence of a sense of self. Erikson would say that
just as the early Americans had Continental and African
roots and did themselves no favor in trying to blot
them out, so later Americans still have family and
cultural histories which they bury at risk to
themselves.

5. Reformers

Erikson has bluntly taken to task the loud
moralizing and proclivity to put all the blame elsewhere of the very reformers whose causes he applauds.
He fears the moralizing of feminists; he is saddened by
American blacks who seek to put all the blame of the
shocking condition of modern American blacks on the
white community. In the seventies, he pointed out that
student opponents of the war in Viet Nam vilified the
entire adult population of their country. His concern
was born in seeing honest and needed reforms becoming

twisted and in need of reform themselves. All this because of an old American temptation, the temptation to divide the world into good guys and bad guys, the reformers taking the risk of becoming just as bigoted as the bigots who originally told them to "stay in their places." We need to know our own history if we want to avoid repeating the dark side of it again and again.

If the early Americans were quick to pick up a rifle or shovel, if they worked at farming and commerce as hard as they worked at fighting, we who come later still share that need to get going. We don't like sitting around talking things over; we want to get to work or to go to war. We need action. Just as our founders revelled in their own newness, we, too, thirst for novelties, fads, and new things. American inventiveness, Yankee ingenuity, is a good thing, unless it is shallow.

6. A New Identity

Erik Erikson calls his fellow Americans to a new Identity, not the old Revolutionary one, characterized by being quick on the trigger, thinking that we are better than everybody else, because down deep we know we really aren't. Not an ingenuity which makes work an end in itself, disregarding reflection and our own history and the needs of our children and adolescents.

Erik Erikson calls the American people to join the whole human race as equals. He calls for a sense of thoughtfulness and reflectiveness to go with our industriousness. He is concerned that we rediscover the meaning of ethics. It is this sense of ethics that is the subject of the last chapter of this book.

106

RECOMMENDED READINGS FOR THIS CHAPTER

Childhood and Society does, indeed, have a chapter
germane to this one. It is Chapter Eight, "Reflections
on the American Identity." It is a trenchant and
powerful piece of work. Sketches of the Americans of
the nineteen forties and the connection between them
and their earlier American ancestors. The Foreword to
the First Edition of this book, repeated in the revised
edition, has an excellent description of the place of
history in psychoanalysis.

Chapter Nine of this introductory work, which you
have just read, is taken in the main from two books,
each containing a series of lectures given by Erikson
in nineteen seventy-two and three. Both these books
are more in the style of lectures than the main body of
Erikson's work. His lecture style is somewhat more
familiar and conversational in tone than the formal
style used in most of his other works. Hence, both are
easier going for the average reader. The books are:
Toys and Reasons (New York, 1975) and Dimensions of a
New Identity (New York, 1974). The second of these is
the most readable of all of Erikson's books, as well as
being short; it is a little over a hundred pages in
length.

As to the world of arts and letters, surely Mark
Twain's Huckleberry Finn is a very American fellow
indeed, as is Twain's Tom Sawyer and A Connecticut
Yankee in the Court of King Arthur. None of these
characters has a whole lot of use for things past or
things European. Mark Twain will have to serve as my
American Shakespeare.

Erikson himself probed into American folk songs
in his search for the American Identity. Such songs
as "John Henry" and "I Wish I Were Single Again" were
helpful to him and might be of use to the reader. The
reference to this search on Erikson's part is
Childhood and Society, Chapter Eight.

Studs Terkel has a book of interviews of contemporary Americans that illustrate almost every facet of
the American character which Erikson discusses.
American Dreams by Studs Terkel.

For Americans as blamers, one might read Arthur
Miller's play, The Crucible or even The Scarlet Letter.

American prejudices--The Autobiography of Malcolm X, Rabbit Run, Huckleberry Finn, The Bell Jar.

Immigrants--The Fortunate Pilgrim by Mario Puzo, The Bread Givers by Anzia Yezierska. The ethic of work, again in Studs Terkel's interviews, Working. There is a never-ending list. We intend here a sample, no more.

CHAPTER X

ETHICS, MUTUALITY AND PEACE

A. Ego, Development and Ethics

  1. Ego Psychology and Ethics

     This chapter is in part a summary of the chapters
that   preceded   it.   Ethical   concerns   run   through
Erikson's thinking from one end to the other. We have
explained E.H.E. as an ego psychologist.   He sees
human life as a developing series of options.   There
is always a pull, at any given stage, between two
central qualities of life, given a person's individuality and historical times.   There is always the
struggle, the dialectic. Make no mistake, he will not
allow in his vision of life a sort of rosy picture with
no dark forces pulling against the vital force of a
given stage; still, he is clear that there are positive
as well as negative forces. Every stage of human life
is marked by a struggle between good and evil.   There
is always an ethical dimension, even if in the beginning it is hidden; even if throughout one's life much
of the ego's work is a part of the unconscious.
Erikson's work concerns itself continually with
uncovering unconscious motivation and thus making
clearer what has determined our choices. Insight into
choices for him implies that some choices are better
than others. A strong ego is a responsible ego.   A
responsible ego implies a sense of continuity in one's
life, an awareness of one's development, one's family's
development, and the history of one's people.

  2. The Development of an Ethical Sense

     Early in human development, the human conscience
arises. We speak here of the age of the toddler, the
pre-schooler, Erikson's Stage Three: Initiative versus
Guilt.   Guilt can mean being guilty. It can be more
than just a feeling of having done something wrong.
An informed guilt puts a rein on initiative.   It
recognizes that unbridled initiative can interfere with
the lives of other people as well as my own.

     Always the developmentalist, Erikson describes the
guilt of the pre-schooler and of the grade school child
as moralism. Moralists build a code of right and wrong
that is based upon threats.   These threats may be
outer in nature, based on a fear of being abandoned or

punished or exposed. They may be inner fears, an inner feeling of being guilty, of feeling abandoned, or feeling exposed. In any case, children are seen as moralists. Their ethical sense is beginning to awake with the birth of conscience. Still, a child is "good" in order to forestall something threatening.

Does youth differ from childhood in an under-standing of right and wrong? Indeed, yes. The age of the crisis of Identity finds the young person who is neither child nor adult striving to find an ideal worth being faithful to. We have described young people in Chapter Six of this book as making their value judgments in an ideological way. We have been reminded that ideologies are by nature always too simple, even the best of them. Ideologies see questions of morality in black and white terms; they do not allow for other shades. In a certain sense, the age of youth is an age committed to ideals that are too simple. There is a certain tunnel vision. It would not be too far off the mark to say that this narrowness is born of lack of experience. The rest of one's life is for finding out the exceptions to the causes of one's youth.

What are the dangers of the Ideological Commitment of Youth? We have another Eriksonian word, Pseudo-species. If it is characteristic of the best of youth to commit itself to a cause, it is also characteristic of youth to regard those without this view of things as belonging to another and lesser species; in short, a pseudospecies. Other visions, other points of view, are regarded as inferior. And so, the world is divided up into true believers and heretics of one kind or another. The task of adulthood is the discovery that there is only one species of human beings, the human species, and that many of the heretics have something to be said for their way of looking at life. In theory, at least, adults are supposed to be more broad-minded than adolescents. The fundamental difference between children and those older is that the morality of children is basically formed from the threat of loss or punishment, whether outer or inner. The morality of youth begins to form an ideal. An adult morality brings breadth to the ideals of youth.

We must not forget that the ideals of youth are closely connected to the authority confusion that is the dark side of ideological commitment. That confusion about authority frequently lasts a long time. It is not dispelled overnight, replaced by an ideal.

And, of course, some people emerge from the Crisis of Identity with the issue of ideals basically unsolved. Nowhere in Erikson's life cycle is one guaranteed a successful emergence from a given stage.

B. Special Issues

1. Male and Female Ethics?

Although Erik Erikson has but one series of stages for men and women alike, he has indicated that men and women do not follow these stages in the same way; he has even indicated that women frequently negotiate the Crisis of Identity and the Crisis of Intimacy at the same time rather than in sequence. He has pointed to mothers as those who not only give birth to babies, but who are primarily the ones responsible for an infant's sense of trust or mistrust. Other authors, primarily Carol Gilligan, have picked up on Erikson's sketch of female Identity formation and have drawn out its ethical implications as well as beginning the task of anchoring their research empirically. Gilligan notes that just as women find Identity and Intimacy at the same time in life, woman's ethical sense is anchored in other people. When I find out what I have got and what I am going to do with it, if I am a woman, I am likely to be concerned about the persons I am going to be doing it with and for. My sense of right and wrong at the age of Identity is far more likely to be concerned with people if I am a woman. Men are more likely to see right and wrong abstractly, just as they are more likely to find Identity first and then look at the more personal dimensions of Intimacy. Male morality is more likely to be divorced from people, more likely to be anchored in principle. Gilligan cites the famous story of Solomon and the two mothers who claimed the same child. Solomon offered to cut the child in two; the mother of the child offered her baby to the false claimant. Solomon's offer is seen as an abstract morality; the mother's as anchored in the baby. Erik Erikson never quite says there is a difference between male and female ethics, but his examples clearly illustrate the difference.

He cites warfare as an example of the folly of men, as we have shown earlier in this book. He warns women against a kind of uncaring birth control. Both these problems concern both sexes, of course. Still, he notes that mothers have hated war as long as they have mourned for their sons who have been

111

sacrificed to it.

The jingoists of history have been mostly men. Not by chance did Virgil long ago open the Aeneid singing of "arms and the man." If women have been bearers of children throughout the ages as men have born arms, there is, says Erikson, a responsibility here as well, an ethical dimension. He finds that dimension to be threatened by modern technological means of birth control. He points out that men can no longer indulge in warfare without threatening us all...and that women have it in their power to put concern for the next generation literally behind them. He almost says that fatherly fathers can no longer be soldiers and that motherly mothers cannot afford to use science to avoid motherhood altogether. In both cases, the virtue at stake is the virtue of care.

Caring is the vital strength he hopes will arise from the struggle between Generativity and Stagnation in the middle years of human life. It is neither a man's virtue nor a woman's but a common strength, hoped for for both. There is, however, a typically male imagination anchored in the male carriage that Erikson sees as more outward than the imagination of women. He finds a proclivity among women anchored in the female carriage for an imagination more inner. Women, for example, are more likely concerned for the inner quality of peace, whereas the male is more likely to dream of conflict and outer exploration. His calling warfare a "male ethical issue", then, is anchored in the male imagination. His calling birth control a woman's ethical issue is anchored not only in the female imagination's centering on inner life, but because the female carries within her the fertilized ovum. Implicit in this shading of ethical issues to one sex or the other is a woman's right to have a public voice in laws concerning the regulation of birth as well as the need for the voices of women as traditional opponents of war to be raised in the public arena as well as the private and more intimate sectors of human living.

Considerations of both war and birth control are primarily issues of caring and they are issues normally decided and presided over by people in the middle years of life. In a portion of an essay on ethics dealing with male and female there should, of course, be_ mention of the ethical concerns regarding intimacies between the sexes. We remind the reader that Erikson's treatment of the stage of Intimacy versus Isolation makes it quite clear that intimacy involves a giving of one's self to another. An approach to intimacy that concerns itself with a multiplication of sexual intimacies, whether with one person or with many, does not add up somehow to Intimacy with a capital "I." Indiscriminate sexual intimacies are often seen as good evidence of an isolated person rather than a loving one, a selfish person rather than a generous one. For Erikson, sex and loving go together as powerful means for human development leading to the universal caring quality he sees as the characteristic of an adult man or woman. Erikson never doubts that adulthood carries with it the responsibility of caring for the world. This includes the small world of home and family, work, and friends and the larger arena of community, state, and the nations of the world. If there is anything sacred in Erik Erikson's ethics, it is the children of the world. Where children are abused by adults or because of adults, he finds ethical decay.

2. Americans and Ethics

Our chapter on the American Identity is loaded with ethical considerations. Robbing children of play-time in the name of "getting ahead" is seen as an American sin; so too, a certain American proclivity to be suspicious of youth's moratorium as a similar waste of time is seen as damaging to successful development. Erikson has pointed out that Americans have been good "blamers" ever since the colonists, however justly, blamed their troubles on the English and King George III of England. The burden of guilt carried by an immigrant people has been seen in the light of trans-ferring the guilt to slaves, women, and Indians. Contrition, certainly an ethical notion, is not an American virtue. In sum, his trenchant comment that loud moralizers have made deals with their own consciences.

3. Play and Ethics

In a very special way, Erikson has pointed to the connection between play and ethics, the danger of the make-believe of childhood extending into adulthood, so that people in responsible places feel free to enter the world of make-believe when accounting for their actions. The American Experience of Watergate had a lot of make-believe in it. Make-believe can be twisted in its usage to mean a license to lie, or worse, to become unable to tell the difference between lies and the truth. Harry Truman's tart comment about Richard Nixon to the effect that Nixon was not so much a liar as a man who couldn't tell the difference between a lie and the truth is here apropos.

Continuing his comments on the connection between play, playfulness and ethics, Erikson points out that the small and playful ritualisms of the daily life of a family or a people are necessary for a sense of continuity in a life. People with no sense of themselves as individuals, members of families and nations are rootless people. Rootless people blow in the wind when confronted with ethical choices. So the small ways in which a family jokes at table, the stories informally told about eccentric uncles, aunts, and clergy, even regionalism and family-isms in speech provide a kind of structure, a sense of knowing who you are and what you and your people stand for that are the base or foundation of an ethical sense.

C. Mutuality: the Golden Rule and Development

And so, every stage in Erikson's eight is a sort of field for struggle between growth and decay. As each stage gives way to another, moralism slowly gives way to idealism, ideology gives way to an adult form of ethics. Erikson is very much a proponent of the very ancient ethical maxim, "Do unto others as you would have others do unto you." ...but he puts it developmentally.

> Understood this way, the Rule would
> say that it is best to do to another
> what will strengthen you even as it
> will strengthen him--that is, what
> will develop his best potentials
> even as it develops yours.

And so, the question of mutuality arises. Erikson does not expect a sense of mutuality from children...if by mutuality one means a concern for other people as well as for one's self. By and large, children's concerns for others are quite pragmatic. They are in business for themselves. When they become youths, they choose ideals and causes; they are concerned for tohers, but narrowly so, quick to judge those not sharing their own slant on things. They are quite intolerant in their newfound ideals. Mutuality is seen as a real concern for every neighbor, as the story of the Good Samaritan pointed out long ago. Nor does it exclude a concern for the self as the ancient writer of Leviticus stated even earlier: "Love thy neighbor as thyself."

Mutuality is not an Eriksonian discovery, surely. E. H. E.'s contribution to the idea of mutuality lies in his insistence that one concern himself or herself with the needs of the other person as an individual and with understanding of where that person is developmentally. Babies don't have the same needs as toddlers. Children don't have the same needs as adults. An enlightened understanding of this Golden Rule, then, looks at the other where he is now. Developmental psychology has cast a strong light on how people differ at different times in their lives. An informed and adult ethics takes this into account. Briefly, it isn't fair to treat kids like grownups...or grownups like kids. The more each of us knows about human development, whether from a study of psychology or from the school of hard knocks, the more likely that one will be able to be truly helpful to one's neighbor.

In the business of interpreting the behavior of others, it's a good idea to know how old they are. Long explanations to five year olds on the beauty of sharing are a waste of time. Lectures to a seventeen year old on settling down could be just as stupid as urging a thirty year old to settle down might be wise. And by the same token, to expect from myself at seventeen what I would see as necessary for me at thirty could be tragic. Developmental psychology tells us that there really is a different set of rules for every age. "One size fits all" simply doesn't go for morality.

D. Transference and Ethics

1. Transference

We have seen then, ego, development, the sexes, the Americans, and playfulness all in an ethical dimension. As this chapter, and with it the book begins to come to a close, the author himself, the interpreter of Erikson, I...have a feeling of uneasiness that my own academic background, so filled with the voice of reason, so devoid of emotion and unconscious elements in human life...has somehow betrayed me.

2. A Personal Aside on the Unconscious

This discussion of ethics seems terribly orderly. As though all a person would have to do to become immediately "ethical" would be to read Chapter Ten of this book, browse a little in the relevant writings of Erik Erikson, perhaps muse a bit, and presto...an "ethical" person. I know this is not the case. I have lived too long and seen the light too many times to believe that reading a book or understanding an idea, no matter how complex, can make me a good person. Something is missing. Something has not been given its due. For want of a better word, I believe that something is the unconscious...mine, yours as reader, and everyone else's. True, at the very first chapter of this book, there is an attempt at elucidating the importance of the unconscious in Erik Erikson's thinking, anchored as it is in the thinking of his predecessor, Sigmund Freud.

Here in a discussion of ethics, I am reminded once again how difficult it is to write well about that vital dimension in the life of every person.

I am reminded of reading a book, filled with footnotes and references, and loaded with fine distinctions on the subject of silence in Judaeo-Christian mysticism. The more words I read and the more footnotes I traced down, the more I realized just how humorous a predicament the author of the book had put himself in. After all, silence is, among other things, an experience of not hearing anyone talking. Talking includes the written word as well as the spoken word. It's hard to talk about not talking.

By the same token, it's hard to write clearly about the unconscious...because I am not conscious of it directly, and neither are you. It is a far-off country that we can read about but not go to. We can have intimations of it from dreams and slips in conversations in the presence of a reliable guide, but we cannot go there.

If the unconscious mind seems very much like death, "the undiscovered country from whose bourne no traveller returns," it has been the task of psychoanalysis in our own time to put order into the hints we all have for its significance in day-to-day living. These very insights can be of help in coming to terms with the age-old human puzzle, "Why do intelligent people of seeming good will so often start wars, beat their children, and look down upon their in-laws, their neighbors and the Russians?"

Part of the answer lies in a lack of awareness. The underworld of the unconscious mind is an active place. That hidden activity is the reason psycho-analysts have been interested in history and literature.

One can often see the motives of people in times past better than in times present. A person's cultural and family history is filled with hints that help to explain today's strengths and weaknesses. The motives of characters in fiction are far more transparent than my own.

3. Transference, Once Again

Freud's discovery of the process of transference is a beautiful example of the workings of the unconscious mind. Transference has lots of ethical overtones. If Luther transformed his childhood hatred for his father to the father figure of the Pope, it is most unlikely that he was aware of that neat trick. It is a measure of Luther's greatness that he chose a father figure on whom to vent his wrath who was very much in need of reform! Old wounds, inflicted by people long since dead or forgotten are routinely transferred to contemporary persons of importance in our own lives. Many a man has tried to even old scores with his childhood's mother by abusing his own wife or his own children. Many a public official has dealt with his own dishonesty by transferring it to defenseless minorities while running on a law-and-order ticket. If you can't put your own house in order, it is amazing how much zeal that can supply you with in shaping up everybody else.

The important thing here is not so much to use a knowledge of unconscious transferences to make a new list of "bad guys" to be dealt with, as it is to remind us that we all transfer early slights, abandonments, and betrayals to later people. Some knowledge of the times of our own childhoods can be powerful hints toward explaining puzzling outbursts directed at innocent people in later life.

Transferences can live on from generation to generation as well. They can persist as malicious cycles for decades and even centuries. Child beaters after all, beget child beaters. The fathers of our

117

cycles for decades and even centuries. Child beaters after all, beget child beaters. The fathers of our country passed their righteous proclivity to blaming others to succeeding generations of Americans. American attitudes toward the Soviets bear a striking resemblance to American attitudes toward the English two hundred years ago. Shakespeare's comment, put in the mouth of Marc Antony, rings through the centuries, "The evil that men do lives after them; the good is oft interred with their bones."

And so, part of the problem of persisting evil in the world lies first in its hidden nature, here exemplified by the psychoanalytic term, transference. If transferences of old scores to be settled have a way of shifting to new people without anybody being aware of it, so it is equally difficult to recognize the passage of such patterns from father to son, from mother to daughter. It is the business of psychoanalysis to reveal this hidden dimension. It is the harsh light of psychoanalytic insight which Erikson has brought to bear on the field of Ethics.

E. Peace

Surely, the issue of peace is the paramount ethical issue of the twentieth century; the survival of civilized life depends upon it. The issue of world peace begins with an informed mutuality on the part of individuals. It extends to such a practice of the Golden Rule on the part of larger bodies of people-- corporations, unions, states and nations. The recognition of the hidden facets of one's own character, as well as the character of one's family and one's people, is surely one of the bases of a mature personal, corporate, and global ethical code. Nations fall for the same kinds of transferential tricks and ignorances of human development that individuals do. It was one of Walt Kelly's inhabitants of the Okeefanokie Swamp who so wisely said, "We have found the enemy, and it is us."

The task of psychoanalytic insight is to enlighten individuals and groups in the study of their own world, national, and personal histories, so that they may have the power and the acumen to avoid repeating the tragedies that befell their own ancestors and the tragedies that they experienced in their own childhoods.

The beginnings of individual and corporate peace lie in recognizing the full dimensions of yesterday's sorrow.

This chapter and this book come to a close with the author's hoping that a near lifetime spent in academic work will not have made him too much of a theoretician and too much of a rationalist in his explanations of the work of a great man. Just as you can kill a great work of art by talking too much about it, so can you also make readers forget the importance of the unconscious by trying too hard to make it all understandable. I have talked enough; the work of reading the book of your own mind remains for you, the reader. And that is harder than reading a book. I'm quite sure that Erik Erikson will agree with me on that one.

THE END

READINGS SUGGESTED BY THIS CHAPTER

Peace is not formally treated in Childhood and Society, nor is ethics as such. I would suggest that the reader of that book read its concluding chapter, entitled, "Conclusion: Beyond Anxiety." The chapter is a drawing together of the central themes of the book, just as this one is.

The main body of this chapter, including the quotation, comes from Insight and Responsibility, which is a formal treatment of the ethical implications of psychoanalysis. I refer the reader as well to a remarkable short passage at the very end of Dimensions of a New Identity, entitled, "Conclusion: A Century of the Adult."

The fullest treatment of peace in Erikson's work remains his life of Mohandas Gandhi, the full title of which is Gandhi's Truth: On the Origins of Militant Non-Violence. It will not surprise the reader at this point to discover that one of Erikson's most trenchant essays on peace is also an essay on woman. See Identity: Youth and Crisis, Chapter VII, "Womanhood and the Inner Space."

As for the field of literature, I have used Margaret Craven's short novel, I heard the Owl Call My Name as an admirable depiction of an ethical man. A horrible description of "male" combativeness can be found in Ursula K. LeGuin's The Word for World is Forest. It would be puckish for me to suggest that a reader searching for embodiments of peace should read through the Gospel according to Luke, or perhaps the book of the Prophet Isaiah, Chapters Thirty to Forty-Five. Failing that, The Communist Manifesto by Karl Marx and Friedrich Engels might shed light on this elusive business. Graham Greene has a recent novel which could be characterized as a combination of The Manifesto and the Gospel, a novel entitled, Monsignor Quixote. Given the frivolous but dead serious tone of these comments, I suggest to the reader of poetry the name of e. e. cummings. For those who prefer capital letters, another poet of peace, Lawrence Ferlinghetti. I should like to close this earnest list with the suggestion that the paintings and mosaics of Marc Chagall would be a fitting recommendation as a commentary on the works about ethics and peace by an author who was once an artist himself, Erik Homburger Erikson.

I will close these suggestions and this book with a gentle hint that the reader might wish to see the Marx Brothers in non-violent action using bologna sausages as weapons...or to watch the caperings of the peaceful mad folk of the French film, The King of Hearts. For the more serious, there is Ben Kingsley in Gandhi, the man Erikson has chosen as his own special personification, however flawed, of peacefulness in the twentieth century.

APPENDICES

APPENDIX A

LIST OF BOOKS AND FILMS

This list contains books and film titles for each chapter of the book. Most of these titles are mentioned in the paragraphs at the end of each chapter. Here they are in fuller form. It is the hope of the author that such a complete listing will make it easier for the reader to identify the recommended works for purchase, borrowing or rental. Films are listed by title and date of issue. Distributors for purchase or rental are given for films.

CHAPTER 1--THE GROUNDPLAN

A. Books

Erik H. Erikson, The Growth of His Work by Robert
Coles. Boston, Little Brown, 1970.

CHAPTER 2--CHILDHOOD

A. Books

A Bird in the House by Margaret Laurence. New
York, Bantam, 1970.

Higglety, Pigglety, Pop by Maurice Sendak. New
York, Harper and Row, 1967.

I Know Why the Caged Bird Sings by Maya Angelou.
New York, Bantam, 1969.

Jacob Two Two Meets the Hooded Fang by Mordecai
Richler. New York, Bantam, 1977.

Jennifer, Hecate, MacBeth, William McKinley and
Me, Elizabeth by E. H. Konigsberg. New York, Atheneum,
Aladin, 1967.

Outside Over There by Maurice Sendak. New York,
Harper and Row, 1981.

Seven Little Monsters by Maurice Sendak. New
York, Harper and Row, 1977.

The Adventures of Tom Sawyer by Mark Twain. New
York, Greystone Press, 1903.

Very Far Away by Maurice Sendak. New York,
Harper and Row, 1957.

Where the Wild Things Are by Maurice Sendak. New
York, Harper and Row, 1963.

B. Films

Everybody Rides the Carrousel. Ann Arbor, MI,
University of Michigan, 1975.

Fanny and Alexander. Wilmette, IL, Films Incorporated, 1983.

Shoeshine. Wilmette, IL, Janus Films, 1946.

CHAPTER 3--YOUTH

A. Books

The Bell Jar by Sylvia Plath. New York, Bantam, 1971.

The Beginning Place by Ursula K. LeGuin. New York, Harper and Row, 1980.

The Bread Givers by Anzia Yezierska. New York, Persea Books, 1925.

The Catcher in the Rye by J. D. Salinger. New York, Bantam, 1951.

Hamlet, Prince of Denmark by William Shakespeare.

In a Different Voice by Carol Gilligan. Cambridge, Harvard University Press, 1982.

I Heard the Owl Call My Name by Margaret Craven. New York, Dell, 1973.

I Know Why the Caged Bird Sings by Maya Angelou. New York, Bantam, 1969.

The Autobiography of Malcolm X. New York Grove Press, 1964.

A Mixture of Frailties by Robertson Davies. New York, Penguin, 1960.

Passages In Teaching by Francis L. Gross, Jr. New York, Philosophical Library, 1982.

The Stone Angel by Margaret Laurence. New York, Penguin, 1964.

The Tombs of Atuan by Ursula K. LeGuin. New York, Bantam, 1975.

Very Far Away from Anywhere Else by Ursula K. LeGuin. New York, Bantam, 1976.

A Wizard of Earthsea by Ursula K. LeGuin. New York, Bantam, 1975.

B. Films

Breaking Away. Wilmette, IL, Films Incorporated, 1979.

Closely Watched Trains. Mt. Vernon, NY, Audio Brandon Films, 1966.

Everybody Rides the Carrousel. Ann Arbor, MI, University of Michigan, 1975.

The Diner. New York, NY, MGM/UA Entertainment Company, 1982.

The Graduate. Mt. Vernon, NY, Audio Brandon Films, 1967.

Gregory's Girl. Great Britain, 1982. (Distributor unavailable.)

Ordinary People. Mt. Vernon, NY, Audio Brandon Films, 1980.

CHAPTER 4--ADULTHOOD

A. Books

1. Intimacy vs. Isolation

The Assistant by Bernard Malamud. New York, Avon, 1957.

The Diviners by Margaret Laurence. New York, Bantam, 1974.

God's Grace by Bernard Malamud. New York, Farrar, Strauss and Giroux, 1982.

I Heard the Owl Call My Name by Margaret Craven. New York, Dell, 1973.

A Jest of God by Margaret Laurence. New York, Knopf, 1966.

Rabbit Run by John Updike. New York, Fawcett Crest, 1978.

The Second Coming by Walker Percy. New York, Pocketbook, 1980.

Sonnets by William Shakespeare.

2. Generativity vs. Stagnation.

The Diviners by Margaret Laurence. New York, Bantam, 1974.

The Fixer by Bernard Malamud. New York, Dell, 1966.

God's Grace by Bernard Malamud. New York, Farrar, Straus and Giroux, 1982.

The Heart of the Matter by Graham Greene. New York, Viking, 1948.

Julius Caesar by William Shakespeare.

MacBeth by William Shakespeare.

Monsignor Quixote by Graham Greene. New York, Simon and Schuster, 1982.

One Flew Over the Cuckoo's Nest by Ken Kesey. New York, Signet, 1962.

Othello the Moor of Venice by William Shakespeare.

The Power and the Glory by Graham Greene. New York, Bantam, 1980.

Rabbit is Rich by John Updike. New York, Fawcett Crest, 1981.

Rabbit Redux by John Updike. New York, Fawcett Crest, 1977.

The Stone Angel by Margaret Laurence. New York, Penguin, 1964.

B. Films

1. Intimacy vs. Isolation

Carnal Knowledge. Mt. Vernon, NY, Audio Brandon Films, 1971.

Goodbye Mr. Chips. Wilmette, IL, Films Incorporated, 1969.

La Dolce Vita. Mt. Vernon, NY, Audio Brandon Films, 1961.

La Strada. Wilmette, IL, Janus Films, 1954.

Lonely Hearts. Australia, 1983.

The Nights of Cabiria. Mt. Vernon, NY, Audio Brandon Films, 1957.

Rachel, Rachel. St. Louis, MO, Swank Motion Pictures, 1968.

2. Generativity vs. Stagnation

The Autobiography of Miss Jane Pittman. Champaign, IL, University of Illinois, 1974.

Carnal Knowledge. Mt. Vernon, NY, Audio Brandon Films, 1971.

Citizen Kane. Wilmette, IL, Films Incorporated, 1941.

Dr. Strangelove. St Louis, MO, Swank Motion Pictures, 1964.

Everybody Rides the Carrousel. Ann Arbor, MI, University of Michigan, 1975.

Fanny and Alexander. Wilmette, IL, Films Incorporated, 1983.

Gandhi. St. Louis, MO, Swank Motion Pictures, 1983.

Kramer vs. Kramer. St. Louis, MO, Swank Motion Pictures, 1979.

One Flew Over the Cuckoo's Nest. New York, NY, United Artists 16, 1976.

Ordinary People. Mt. Vernon, NY, Audio Brandon Films, 1980.

CHAPTER 5--OLD AGE

A. Books

Kinds of Love by May Sarton. New York, Norton, 1980.

King Lear by William Shakespeare.

The Stone Angel by Margaret Laurence. New York, Penguin, 1964.

B. Films

The Autobiography of Miss Jane Pittman. Champaign, IL, University of Illinois, 1974.

Everybody Rides the Carrousel. Ann Arbor, MI, University of Michigan, 1975.

Fanny and Alexander. Wilmette, IL, Films Incorporated, 1983.

Harry and Tonto. Wilmette, IL, Films Incorporated, 1974.

On Golden Pond. St. Louis, MO, Swank Motion Pictures, 1981.

Wild Strawberries. Wilmette, IL, Janus Films, 1957.

CHAPTER 6--YOUTH

See Chapter 2 for book and film listing.

CHAPTER 7--PLAY, TOYS, AND WORK

A. Books

Twelfth Night by William Shakespeare.

Where the Wild Things Are by Maurice Sendak. New York, Harper and Row, 1963.

Working by Studs Terkel. New York, Pantheon, 1982.

Zorba the Greek by Nikos Kazantzakis. New York, Ballantine Books, 1952.

For play and toys, see books listed under Chapter 2.

B. Films

Butch Cassidy and the Sundance Kid. Wilmette, IL, Films Incorporated, 1969.

Movies of the Marx Brothers.

Zorba the Greek. Wilmette, IL, Films Incorporated, 1964.

CHAPTER 8--MALE AND FEMALE

A. Books

Don Quixote by Miguel De Cervantes. New York, Penguin, 1614.

The Gospel According to Luke.

In a Different Voice by Carol Gilligan. Cambridge, Harvard University Press, 1982.

The Seasons of a Man's Life by Daniel Levinson, et al. New York, Knopf, 1978.

The Stone Angel by Margaret Laurence. New York, Penguin, 1964.

The Tombs of Atuan by Ursula K. LeGuin. New York, Bantam, 1975.

Very Far Away from Anywhere Else by Ursula K. LeGuin. New York, Bantam, 1976.

A Wizard of Earthsea by Ursula K. LeGuin. New York, Bantam, 1975.

The Word for World is Forest by Ursula K. LeGuin. New York, Berkley Medallion, 1972.

B. Films

Dr. Strangelove. St. Louis, MO, Swank Motion Pictures, 1964.

Kramer vs. Kramer. St. Louis, MO, Swank Motion Pictures, 1979.

La Strada. Wilmette, IL, Janus Films, 1954.

On Golden Pond. St. Louis, MO, Swank Motion Pictures, 1981.

Rachel, Rachel. Mt. Vernon, NY, Audio Brandon Films, 1968.

Wild Strawberries. Wilmette, IL, Janus Films, 1957.

CHAPTER 9--THE AMERICAN IDENTITY

A. Books

American Dreams, Lost and Found by Studs Terkel. New York, Ballantine, 1980.

The Bread Givers by Anzia Yezierska. New York, Persea Books, 1925.

A Connecticut Yankee in the Court of King Arthur by Mark Twain. New York, Harper and Brothers, 1889.

The Crucible by Arthur Miller. New York, Bantam, 1953.

The Fortunate Pilgrim by Mario Puzo. New York, Fawcett, 1978.

The Grapes of Wrath by John Steinbeck. New York, Compass, 1939.

The Adventures of Huckleberry Finn by Mark Twain. New York, Grosset and Dunlop, 1948.

The Scarlet Letter by Nathaniel Hawthorne. Columbus, Ohio State University Press, 1962.

The Adventures of Tom Sawyer by Mark Twain. New York, Greystone Press, 1922.

Working by Studs Terkel. New York, Pantheon, 1982.

B. Films

The Grapes of Wrath. Wilmette, IL, Films Incorporated, 1940.

The Emigrants. St. Louis, MO, Swank Motion Pictures, 1972.

CHAPTER 10--ETHICS, MUTUALITY AND PEACE

A. Books

The Autobiography of Malcolm X. New York, Grove Press, 1964.

A Coney Island of the Mind by Lawrence Ferlinghetti. New York, New Directions, 1958.

The Communist Manifesto by Karl Marx and Fredrich Engels. New York, Pelican, 1967.

Don Quixote by Miguel De Cervantes. New York, Penguin, 1970.

The Gospel According to Luke.

The Adventures of Huckleberry Finn by Mark Twain. New York, Grosset and Dunlop, 1948.

Isaiah, Chapters 30-45.   The Book of Consolation.

One Flew Over the Cuckoo's Nest by Ken Kesey.
New York, Signet, 1962.

Passages in Teaching by Francis L. Gross, Jr.
New York, Philosophical Library, 1982.

The Scarlet Letter by Nathaniel Hawthorne.
Columbus, Ohio State University Press, 1962.

Starting from San Francisco by Lawrence
Ferlinghetti.   New York, New Directions, 1967.

100 Selected Poems by e. e. cummings.

The Word for World is Forest by Ursula K. LeGuin.
New York, Berkley Medallion, 1972.

B. Films

Dr. Strangelove.   St. Louis, MO, Swank Motion
Picture, 1964.

Gandhi.   St. Louis, MO, Swank Motion Pictures,
1983.

The King of Hearts.   New York, NY, Australian
Information Source, 1967.

Movies of the Marx Brothers.

One Flew Over the Cuckoo's Nest.   New York, NY,
United Artists 16, 1976.

APPENDIX B

BOOKS AND ARTICLES BY ERIK ERIKSON

1. A Chronology Of Erikson's Books:

1950 Childhood and Society (Second Edition, 1963)

1958 Young Man Luther

1959 Identity and the Life Cycle (Reissued in 1980)

1964 Insight and Responsibility

1968 Identity, Youth and Crisis

1969 Gandhi's Truth

1974 Dimensions of a New Identity

1975 Life History and the Historical Moment

1976 Toys and Reasons

1982 The Life Cycle Completed

All of these books are published by W.W. Norton and Company of New York.

2. Other Works By Erikson Referred To In This Book:

1. 1978 "Reflections on Dr. Borg's Life Cycle." In Adulthood, edited by Erik H. Erikson, pp. 1-31, New York, W.W. Norton, 1978.

2. 1981 "On Generativity and Identity," coauthored by Joan M. Erikson, Harvard Educational Review, 51, 249, 1981.

3. 1981 "The Galilean Sayings and the Sense of 'I'." The Yale Review, 70, 321, 1981.

4. 1983   "A Conversation with Erik Erikson,
           by Elizabeth Hall. _Psychology
           Today_, 22, June, 1983.

APPENDIX C

ERIKSON'S CHART OF THE LIFE CYCLE

THE LIFE CYCLE

	1	2	3	4	5	6	7	8
VIII								INTEGRITY vs. DESPAIR
VII							GENERATIVITY vs. STAGNATION	
VI						INTIMACY vs. ISOLATION		
V	Temporal Perspective vs. Time Confusion	Self-Certainty vs. Self-Consciousness	Role Experimentation vs. Role Fixation	Apprenticeship vs. Work Paralysis	IDENTITY vs. IDENTITY CONFUSION	Sexual Polarization vs. Bisexual Confusion	Leader- and Followership vs. Authority Confusion	Ideological Commitment vs. Confusion of Values
IV				INDUSTRY vs. INFERIORITY				
III			INITIATIVE vs. GUILT					
II		AUTONOMY vs. SHAME, DOUBT						
I	TRUST vs. MISTRUST							

139

EXPLAINING THE CHART OF THE LIFE CYCLE

The eight stages are arranged as running diagonally from the lower left corner to the top right corner of the rectangular figure. The horizontal line running across the rectangle consists of various aspects of the stage of Identity.

The crisis of Identity is understood as a renegotiating of all the stages that have preceded it, i.e., Trust vs. Mistrust, Autonomy vs. Shame and Doubt, Initiative vs. Guilt, and Industry vs. Inferiority. Each of these past crises surfaces in a new way in the crisis of Identity. This new form is written on the chart directly over the old form. For example: Self-certainty vs. Self-consciousness is a new form of the crisis of Autonomy vs. Shame and Doubt. So, the crisis of the two year old occurs again in adolescence. Adolescence of course is the time of the crisis of Identity.

If adolescence means a renegotiation of the earlier crises of childhood, it also anticipates or looks forward to the crises of adulthood, which are yet to come. Therefore Sexual Polarization vs. Bisexual Confusion is an anticipation or preview of the yet to come crisis of Intimacy vs. Isolation. Leader-and Followership vs. Authority Confusion looks forward to the later crisis of Generativity vs. Stagnation. Lastly, Ideological Commitment vs. Confusion of Values looks forward to Integrity vs. Despair.

See the Table of Contents for explanations of each stage in the Life Cycle. The aspects of the crisis of Identity are listed in the Table of Contents under III, D and VI, A, B, and C.

INDEX